INTO THE BREACH AT PUSAN

CAMPAIGNS & COMMANDERS

GREGORY J. W. URWIN, SERIES EDITOR

INTO THE BREACH AT PUSAN

The 1st Provisional Marine Brigade in the Korean War

KENNETH W. ESTES

UNIVERSITY OF OKLAHOMA PRESS : NORMAN

Also by Kenneth W. Estes

Marines under Armor: The Marine Corps and the Armored Fighting Vehicle, 1916–2000 (Annapolis, Md., 2000)
Marine Officer's Guide, 7th ed. (Annapolis, Md., 2008)
U.S. Marines in Iraq 2004–2005: Into the Fray (Washington, D.C., 2011)

This book is published with the generous assistance of The McCasland Foundation, Duncan, Oklahoma.

Library of Congress Cataloging-in-Publication Data

Estes, Kenneth W.
    Into the Breach at Pusan : the 1st Provisional Marine Brigade in the Korean War / Kenneth W. Estes.
        p.   cm. — (Campaigns and commanders ; v. 31)
    Includes bibliographical references and index.
    ISBN 978-0-8061-4254-8 (hardcover : alk. paper)
    1. Korean War, 1950–1953—Regimental histories—United States. 2. United States. Marine Corps. Provisional Marine Brigade, 1st. 3. Korean War, 1950–1953—Campaigns—Korea (South)—Pusan region. I. Title.
    DS919.E77 2012
    951.904'242—dc23

                                                                2011050479

Into the Breach at Pusan: The 1st Provisional Marine Brigade in the Korean War is volume 31 in the Campaigns and Commanders series.

The paper in this book meets the guidelines for permanence and durability of the Committee on Production Guidelines for Book Longevity of the Council on Library Resources, Inc. ∞

1 2 3 4 5 6 7 8 9 10

For Geneviève

Once more unto the breach, dear friends, once more,
Or close the wall up with our English dead!
In peace there's nothing so becomes a man
As modest stillness and humility;
But when the blast of war blows in our ears,
Then imitate the action of the tiger:
Stiffen the sinews, summon up the blood.

Shakespeare, *Henry V* (5.3.44–51)

CONTENTS

ILLUSTRATIONS

PREFACE AND
ACKNOWLEDGMENTS

The story of the 1st Provisional Marine Brigade in the Korean War represents the essential marine corps epic. The invasion of the Republic of South Korea by the North Koreans caught the Western world by surprise. The brigade sailed to Korea among the very first reinforcements sent out from the United States once President Harry S. Truman ordered U.S. forces into action. By the time it arrived, the beleaguered United Nations forces were fighting literally with their backs to the sea, covering the last ports remaining in friendly hands. Drawing upon traditional marine corps discipline, training, and fighting spirit, the men of the brigade defeated their opponents in each of the three counteroffensive battles into which they were ordered. After a month of intermittent fighting in the Pusan Perimeter, the brigade reboarded its assault ships and sailed into the setting sun, to yet another battle now etched in marine corps lore: Inchon. Much can be learned about the marine corps as a service and as a part of the American military establishment by studying the events of and circumstances surrounding the deployment and operations of the brigade.

While serving as an officer in the U.S. Marine Corps, I naturally became immersed in the lore surrounding the marine brigade in the Pusan Perimeter. As I note in the last chapter, the example of the brigade's being hurriedly organized and dispatched to a new war with no advance notice was repeatedly drummed into us by our seniors. They told us that one never knew when we would be called upon

to "mount out" to an unfamiliar clime and place, to confront an
enemy heretofore unknown. Although generally presumed to be a
forgotten battle in the so-called Forgotten War, the Pusan Perimeter
fight of the 1st Provisional Marine Brigade remained hallowed in
the corps, even though the later events of the Korean War tended to
overshadow it.

When the time came to make my first serious efforts in Marine
Corps history, I researched various themes regarding the marine corps
and the Korean War.[1] While I was pleased to find that the official
history volumes provided much frank and revealing detail of the initial
mobilization and conduct of the various campaigns, there remained
many questions yet to be answered. However, investigation of secondary works related to the marine corps in Korea revealed surprisingly
little new material. On the contrary, one frequently encountered
contradictions: for example, one source asserted that marine corps
aircraft proved more effective in ground support missions because
they were "Corsairs, piloted by men who were ground officers."[2]
The oft-repeated refrain that most of the officers and 65 percent of
the noncommissioned officers of the marine brigade were combat
veterans seemed facile, as most corporals to technical sergeants in
1950 would have enlisted after 1944, and thus had little likelihood
of entering combat before World War II ended.[3] And did American
and South Korean troops face "almost overwhelming odds" or the
"sadly understrength" North Koreans?[4] Was the 5th Marine Regiment "a formidable combat unit," or was it predictably green at its
introduction to combat in the Pusan Perimeter?[5]

It also became clear to me that writers had been using the same
published sources and referring to the same after-action reports held
in Quantico libraries (now the Gray Research Center) and the USMC
Historical Division as the last word in documentation. However,
the reports were written with varied attention to detail merely a
day or two after the conclusion of the events and while their authors
were distracted by the pending landings at Inchon. The usual organizational war diaries or staff journals, which one might normally
count upon for spontaneity if not depth, did not survive the passage of
time. Other studies written even later are colored by the interservice
rivalries that have plagued the U.S. armed services in the decades
following the end of World War II.

Apart from resolving the discrepancies found in various published works, I sensed that a fresh investigation might bring interesting new views of this epic campaign. Many previous writers spent too much time bemoaning the unpreparedness of the nation for the war, fighting polemical battles against the political leadership to the extent that the real story of the operations seemed almost lost. It became clear that the Pusan Perimeter campaign loomed much larger than most marine corps observers realized at the time, and was really the U.S. Eighth Army's finest hour, still unheralded. Yet the interservice rivalries stand out in most accounts. A close examination reveals considerable cooperation by all units and services directly engaged at Pusan.

Thus, I decided that we still lacked a balanced approach to the story of the 1st Marine Brigade in the Pusan Perimeter. It remains my chief finding that the marine corps' efforts in the Pusan Perimeter fighting did not "save the army," as marine historians have claimed, but did in fact contribute significantly to the Eighth Army's successful defense of the perimeter. A new and untried unit deployed on short notice to the fighting front, the marine brigade turned in a superb performance that, in and of itself, deserves to be remembered in marine corps annals and enshrined in its traditions.

My research method remained simple. I closely read the after-action reports of the subordinate units as well as the major commands, noting discrepancies and searching for further illumination. The army official history and the war diaries of the Eighth Army and the 24th and 25th Infantry Divisions provided much-needed context. Interesting new material lay in unpublished and previously unused archival sources, especially the classified files of Headquarters Marine Corps now held by the National Archives. The Marine Corps Historical Division delivered pleasant surprises in the form of unpublished and largely unknown diaries of two key marine corps generals who shaped the campaign. These and other previously unused sources led to a more balanced accounting that reflects well on the performance of the 1st Provisional Marine Brigade while providing a deeper understanding of the historical context of their campaign.

While I toiled over the history of the 1st Provisional Marine Brigade from 2007 to 2010, three new works reached the bookstores treating the same subject, at least in part. It would seem that the

Korean War has long ceased to be "forgotten." It remains my opinion that these works have not portrayed adequately the history of the campaign.[6]

Many persons and institutions assisted me in the preparation of this book. My early contact with the men of the August 1950 A Company, 1st Tank Battalion revealed to me some of the first myths of the brigade; for instance, that it reputedly contained the best and most experienced men from 1st Marine Division at Camp Pendleton who could draw on their Pacific War experience to vanquish the North Koreans. Sharing bread, stories, and some libations with Max English, Granville G. Sweet, Joseph Sleger, Donald Gagnon, and other tank commanders convinced me that they were just regular guys swept up in the call to arms, an experience that could have befallen any of us at any point in our service. In the process, I became a close collaborator with the historian of marine corps operations, Oscar E. Gilbert. Ed Gilbert and I have exchanged research and insights for over a decade to great benefit for both of us. Jack Buck, a major of marines and aide-de-camp to General Craig in the Pusan campaign, assisted me to a considerable extent. Merrill Bartlett, Puget Sound neighbor, fellow marine corps officer, and frequent collaborator in historical matters, helped me indirectly by sharing his perilous trials as he strove to assist the former battalion commander of 3rd Battalion, 5th Marines in writing his wartime memoirs. At the National Archives and Records Administration I benefited, as always, from the insights and assistance of Timothy Nenninger, chief of Modern Military Records and past president of the Society for Military History; Patrick Osborne and Barry Zerby of his staff; and Herbert Rawlings-Milton, the supervisory archivist handling my petition for a mandatory declassification review of classified files. At the Marine Corps Historical Division, I received careful assistance from the Reference Section gang: Danny A. Crawford, Robert V. Aquilina, Lena M. Kaljot, Annette Amerman, Kara Newcomer, and Shelia Boyd. I also enjoyed the camaraderie and shared knowledge of Richard Camp, the division's deputy director (2006–2007); Charles Melson, chief historian; and Fred Allison, oral historian, including the latter's essential dissertation on marine corps fighter-bomber doctrine. Gregory Urwin, professor of history at Temple University and editor of this series, first invited me to propose a Korean War study, and Charles Rankin, editor in chief of University of Oklahoma Press, joined him in a major demonstration of confidence and collegiality while I toiled too long in the creation of this work. Emily Jerman, manuscript editor, and Steven Weingartner, copyeditor, performed excellent feats to improve the content, context, and readability of my original manuscript. The Marine Corps Heritage Foundation supported me with a grant in 2005, administered by Charles R. Smith of the Marine Corps Historical Division.

ABBREVIATIONS

APC	Armor Piercing, Capped
AT	Antitank
CAP	Combat Air Patrol
CINCFE	Commander in Chief Far East
CINCPACFLT	Commander in Chief Pacific Fleet
CG	Commanding General
C/S	Chief of Staff
CMC	Commandant of the Marine Corps
CVE	Escort Carrier
CNO	Chief of Naval Operations
EUSAK	U.S. Eighth Army Korea
FEAF	Far Eastern Air Forces
FECOM	Far East Command
FMFPAC	Fleet Marine Force Pacific
GRC	Gray Research Center
HEAT	High Explosive Antitank
HVAP	High Velocity Armor Piercing
JCS	Joint Chiefs of Staff
KIA	Killed in Action
KPA	Korean People's Army
LSD	Landing Ship Dock
MAGTF	Marine Corps Air-Ground Task Force
MAG	Marine Aircraft Group

MarDiv	Marine Division
MGCIS	Marine Ground Control Intercept Squadron
MTACS	Marine Tactical Air Control Squadron
MAW	Marine Aircraft Wing
MIA	Missing in Action
NARA	National Archives and Records Administration
RCT	Regimental Combat Team
ROK	Republic of Korea (Armed Forces)
SAR	Special Action Report
TAC	Tactical Air Control
VMF	Marine Fighter Squadron
VMF(N)	Marine Night Fighter Squadron
VMO	Marine Observation Squadron
WIA	Wounded in Action

Into the Breach at Pusan

1

THE MARINE CORPS AND THE KOREAN CRISIS OF 1950

In the latter half of June 1950, with the outbreak of America's first major conflict of the Cold War just days away, personnel attached to U.S. Marine Corps headquarters in Washington, D.C., were looking backward rather than forward. These staff officers had their attention fixed on the ceremony that would commemorate the seizure of the fort at Derna on 4 July 1805 by a handful of leathernecks and a small army of Mediterranean mercenaries—the feat immortalized by the line "to the shores of Tripoli" in the opening stanza of the "Marines' Hymn." The commander of the U.S. Navy's Sixth Fleet planned to send some of his marines to dedicate a plaque at that site, still known to locals as "the American fort," heralding that occasion as "the first return of marines to the scene of this triumph."[1]

In short, no one in the marine corps anticipated that within two months' time several thousand of its men, organized into the 1st Marine Provisional Brigade, would be fighting a determined enemy in mortal combat in a distant Asian nation, the Republic of Korea. The story of how the marine corps met that challenge has formed an enduring part of its history, culture, and traditions. However, establishing the history of this opening campaign by the marine corps in the Korean War requires a more open and balanced telling, in more realistic terms, than one usually finds in the official histories and other postwar publications. The 1st Provisional Marine Brigade formed part of a large reinforcement effort by the U.S. armed forces,

sent at the war's outset to turn back the invasion of the Republic of
Korea (South Korea) by forces of the Democratic People's Republic
of Korea (North Korea). Although little indication emerges from
marine corps reports, considerable efforts by many combat units
fighting at the same time as the marine brigade were needed to save
the Republic of South Korea from catastrophe in the beginning stages
of the conflict.

There are a number of myths—or at least exaggerations—concerning the 1st Provisional Marine Brigade and its operations in the
Pusan Perimeter. The official history is especially problematic in
that regard, "informing" readers that the brigade had a large proportion of World War II combat veterans; that it was the "fire brigade"
that saved the U.N. Command and the U.S. Eighth Army from
destruction; and that it first validated the air-ground team concept
of the postwar marine corps.

None of these assertions is true. By 1950, few marines at or below
the rank of sergeant were veterans of the previous war, and even some
staff sergeants had enlisted in 1945, too late to see the last marine
corps battles of the Pacific War. As well, the brigade's three infantry
battalion commanders and several of its company commanders
lacked wartime experience commanding troops in the field, instead
serving in ships' detachments and elsewhere. During the battle for
the Pusan Perimeter, at least five regimental-sized "fire brigades"
were fed into the lines in order to sustain the quasi-mobile defense
conducted by the Eighth Army's commander, Lieutenant General
Walton H. Walker; the marine brigade was only one of these. Nor
did the brigade take part in the early and most desperate stages of
the fighting, arriving on the scene only after the initial assaults by
North Korean forces had been repulsed and the defenders had gained
numerical superiority. What's more, the marine brigade never fought
at under 90 percent strength, whereas the army infantry regiments
frequently were at 50 to 60 percent "effectiveness." General Walker,
because of his unfortunate death in at the end of the year (he was
killed in a traffic accident on 23 December, just north of Seoul),
never received deserved recognition as commander of an army that
saved itself at Pusan. As for air-ground team innovation, the brigade
fought a mere twelve days on the ground during the period 6 August
to 5 September 1950, whereas the two day fighter squadrons flew
almost every day throughout the Pusan Perimeter campaign, and sortied

with aircraft flown by aggressive pilots who would bomb and strafe anywhere there were targets. These sorties mostly supported the Eighth Army, not solely the brigade, as asserted in the official history.

In the interests of using a balanced approach, one must begin with an assessment of the state of the marine corps on the eve of this crisis and the ensuing conflict; evaluate the conduct of the month-long campaign; and then assess the telling of the tale, so to speak, as well as the background with which it came to be told in the official narratives.

At the same time that planning for the Derna commemoration was underway, the marine corps struggled to maintain a training regimen and study new organizations in the event of hoped-for budget increases. These measures were some of several responses to the stark reductions in the American defense establishment that had taken place since the end of World War II. For some in the corps, though, the future had begun to look a little brighter in the spring of 1950.

Toward a Force in Readiness

Lieutenant Colonel George R. Newton watched with satisfaction as his marines of 1st Battalion, 5th Marine Regiment (or "5th Marines") filed into their barracks at Camp Pendleton in mid-May 1950. A thirty-five-year-old Naval Academy graduate, Newton had spent World War II as a prisoner of the Japanese—a fate that had overtaken him on the war's first day when his unit, B Company of the American embassy guard detachment in Peking, China, was forced to surrender without firing a shot. Repatriated and returned to active duty in 1946, he had received postwar schooling and commanded a marine barracks and then a service support group before reporting to the battalion in January 1950. Pleased with his new assignment, he was further heartened by developments in the marine corps, which seemed to be emerging from the doldrums of postwar demobilization. The 5th Marines, recently reformed to become the first complete regiment to be restored to service in the 1st Marine Division, was proof that the corps was changing for the better after a period of decline. From Newton's standpoint, things were looking up.[2]

Newton's positive view was reinforced by the regiment's performance in an amphibious landing exercise dubbed Demon III. Conducted in mid-May 1950 on the beaches of Camp Pendleton, California (the

5th Marines' home base), Demon III had a twofold purpose: to demonstrate the marines' ship-to-shore capabilities to visiting students from the Army Command and General Staff College in Fort Leavenworth, Kansas; and, most importantly, to provide the marines with much-needed training in the fundamentals of their trade. The exercise was a success, with all hands turning in an impressive performance; and upon its conclusion Newton stood outside one of the 1st Battalion's barracks and watched with justifiable satisfaction as his men went inside for a much-needed rest. Furthest from his mind at this point was the prospect of returning to Asia to wage war against a fierce and triumphant enemy.

Another cause for optimism was the performance of Marine Fighter Squadron 214 (VMF-214) in Demon III. Famously known as "The Black Sheep Squadron"—the nickname a legacy of the Pacific War, when it compiled an outstanding combat record under the command of the legendary Major Gregory "Pappy" Boyington—VMF-214 had flown its Chance Vought F4U-4B Corsair fighters off the escort carriers USS *Badoeng Strait* and USS *Sicily* to conduct mock close air support attacks for Newton's battalion. The squadron's commander, Lieutenant Colonel Howard A. "Rudy" York led a finely honed group of trained and experienced pilots, all of whom, like himself, had flown combat missions from island bases and carriers in the Pacific War. Since July 1949, York had commanded the "Black Sheep" and imprinted the close air support of ground troops as a sixth sense among his band of veterans. The squadron's deep pilot experience had a simple cause: the corps had stopped recruiting and training pilots after the war, relying on its surplus to fill regular and reserve units alike. These veterans would provide a key advantage within the next few months.[3]

But the high quality of the units taking part in Demon III was the exception rather than the rule for the marine corps in the immediate postwar period. The demobilization of many formations following the end of the war coupled with occupation duties in both Japan and China had drastically eroded the corps' war-fighting capabilities. Attendant to these developments, and contributing to the corps' decline, were losses in experienced personnel and material shortages. Defense reorganization initiatives undertaken during this postwar period had also introduced institutional pressures of no mean import.

The end of World War II in September 1945 found most of the marine corps, then some 458,000 strong, deployed in the Western Pacific Theater with the operating forces of Fleet Marine Force, Pacific (FMFPAC), then consisting of III and V Amphibious Corps, totaling six marine divisions and four marine aircraft wings. Almost half of the corps, however, continued to serve in the traditional shore establishment organizations of security guard barracks for naval stations and bases, and as shipboard detachments on every battleship, aircraft carrier, and cruiser in the U.S. Navy.

Apart from demobilization concerns, the duties of Fleet Marine Force units consisted of disarming Japanese forces and occupying parts of Japan and China. Postwar planning centered on a ready force of two divisions and two aircraft wings, plus an adequate supporting establishment, balanced between the East and West Coast bases, for duty primarily with the Atlantic and Pacific fleets. Marines quickly terminated their occupation duties in Japan, but the deployments in China dragged on into early 1947, with a reprise in 1949 as the Chinese Communists under Mao Tse-Tung (Mao Zedong in modern transliteration) triumphed in the country's civil war. Nevertheless, by the end of 1946 barely fifteen thousand marines remained on the Fleet Marine Force rolls in the Pacific, and an even smaller number in the fledgling Atlantic counterpart.

The corps' great wartime expansion and the service of its divisions with the field armies and corps of the U.S. Army left no doubt in the minds of marine corps leaders that their service would fight in any future global conflict involving the United States. Postwar war plans emerged slowly as the tensions in Europe increased. In 1947, American planning focused on the first twelve to eighteen months of a general war with the Soviet Union. By 1948, the plans included sending a marine division and an army infantry division to Sicily. The first strategic offensive after the outbreak of war would launch eight British and twelve American divisions into the Persian Gulf, aimed at recovering oil fields presumably captured by the Soviets. These offensive moves both specified and implied marine corps tasks that would undoubtedly result in combat with first-line units of the Red Army.[4] By the end of 1949, a new series of war plans provided for the commitment of marine corps formations to continental European battlefields.[5] None of this could happen, however, if the U.S. Marine Corps ceased to exist as a military organization. Marine corps history and lore has reflected various attempts to extinguish it, mostly at the hands of the army and navy.

The "defense reorganization" of 1946–47 instituted the modern American defense establishment, including a U.S. Marine Corps oriented to service with the fleet and maintaining an amphibious warfare capability that it continues to guard jealously to this day. However, some of the marine corps leaders sensed too much critical scrutiny of the corps during the formative process of the legislation. A circle of advocates worked feverishly to counter perceived intentions of the army and air force to strip the ground and aviation elements of the corps away from the Navy Department to swell their own ranks and institutional prowess. A number of staff operatives searched for and provided information deemed crucial to legislative branch staffers and members, perhaps earning the oft-quoted charge by President Truman (who was judged by some to be an "enemy" of the corps) that "the only propaganda machine that rivals that of Stalin is that of the United States Marine Corps."[6]

The National Security Act of 1947, which theoretically unified the U.S. armed forces, contained several key points that could have proven reassuring to the marine corps had there been no pre-existing hard feelings from the conduct of the Pacific War campaigns and the defense reorganization debates. The legislation recognized the corps as an independent service within the Department of the Navy, and identified the Fleet Marine Force as both ground and aviation units organized for seizing and defending advanced naval bases, and for conducting land operations incident to naval campaigns. Accordingly, the marine corps received primary responsibility for the development of doctrine, tactics, techniques, and equipment for amphibious operations, even though the army had conducted more of these in the last war than the corps.

Perceptions of efforts to dissolve the marine corps were not without foundation. Well before the Korean War began, the corps had experienced significant difficulties keeping itself intact. These difficulties were linked not only with interservice squabbling over roles and missions, but also to budgetary concerns. The legendary "reprieve" for the corps in the National Security Act brought no parallel fiscal relief, and the skeletal state of the Fleet Marine Force declined to its postwar nadir. The combat strength of the corps fell in 1948 to eleven understrength battalions of infantry, when each of its two divisions should have fielded nine. As the last battalions performing occupation duty in China returned to the United States, the corps further reduced the existing 1st and 2nd Marine Divisions to a mere three infantry battalions (each representing a cadre infantry regiment) and a single company of amphibious tractors (or "amtracs"). Similarly, tank battalions were scaled down to a single company equipped with obsolete M4A3 Sherman medium tanks. In World War II, by way contrast, these divisions had each boasted three regiments totaling nine infantry battalions as well as attached battalions of tanks and amtracs. Aviation strength held at eighteen active squadrons of fighter, transport, and observation aircraft backed by thirty reserve fighter squadrons.[7]

At the same time, however, there were hopeful signs of resurgence in the Fleet Marine Force. With the return of the forces from China and Guam, sufficient personnel could be gathered to reform a complete 5th Marines of three infantry battalions in the 1st Marine Division, while fiscal year funding for 1950 would enable the divisions to expand under a new table of organization in which two of the three infantry regiments would be manned. Thus, the 5th Marines reformed during September 1949 at Camp Pendleton under the command of Colonel Victor H. Krulak with the first two battalions to return from overseas service.

Krulak, a protégé of Fleet Marine Force commander (as of June 1950) and future commandant Lieutenant General Lemuel C. Shepherd, had won a Navy Cross in late 1943 on Choiseul in the Solomon Islands chain while leading a raid with his 2nd Parachute Battalion prior to the Bougainville assault. Stories of Krulak's tough demeanor and piercing manner in handling his officers and in inspecting his troops were legion. There seems little doubt that Krulak's character and command style were well-suited for guiding the 5th Marines through a grueling regimen of training and exercises. Under the new division commander, the equally tough, brainy, and brusque Major General Graves B. Erskine, the 1st Marine Division began to sharpen its combat skills after the years of postwar uncertainty.

Aviation remained least affected by the imbroglio in China. The pilot surplus at the end of World War II had posed initial personal hardships when it came time to thin the corps' ranks, but the active and reserve squadrons remained filled with combat veterans, to the extent that the recruiting of new pilots ceased until 1950.

By 1949, the thirty reserve squadrons all flew the same F4U-4B variant of the superb Corsair fighter and had also adapted to the same air-ground support tactics as did the regulars, thus conforming to the system devised in 1945 in the final stages of the Western Pacific Campaign. At twenty-two reserve bases, sixteen hundred veteran pilots flew their fighters on weekends and at other opportunities. A typical squadron mustered forty-seven pilots (two more than authorized) and had a waiting list of equally capable veterans eager to join. The pilots maintained their combat skills and the corps was able to draw on wartime stocks to keep its Corsairs in fighting trim. In addition, the pilots cycled through marine corps professional schools and duty assignments with ground and administrative organizations—which had not been possible in wartime—thus bonding them anew to their service.

As the commander of Marine Aircraft Group 12 remarked later, "All of the pilots were ex-World War II guys; most of them had been doing nothing but flying fighters since they came into the Marine Corps, let's say 1942. So these guys had been eight years doing nothing but flying fighters, and they were good. They were real pros. These were the first pilots that went to Korea."[8]

Standing in solitary contrast to the overall positive state of the marine corps aviation arm was the unsatisfactory progress made to date with the development and employment of helicopters. The 1946 Special Board laid down theoretical requirements for helicopters for conducting amphibious landings from dispersed anchorages in the dawning era of nuclear weapons. The experimental helicopter squadron HMX-1 began operations in 1947, evaluating helicopters initially intended as replacements for half of the OY-type light liaison and observation planes. The following year, the first Sikorsky HO3S "Dragon-fly" and Piasecki HRP helos met the stated requirements for utility use. However, the 1949 Marine Corps Equipment Board recommended that the follow-on HRP-1 be rejected as a transport helicopter.

The helicopters on hand had suffered from their use, however. The six HRPs of HMX-1 required overhaul in mid-1950, and two HRP-1 helos already overhauled had been assigned to navy use as antisubmarine aircraft. Two new production HRP-2 helos would arrive in June 1950, with no further deliveries in fiscal year 1951 yet scheduled. The Plans and Programs director conceded that without a vibrant helicopter program "the Marine Corps has little to offer as its contribution to military progress since the end of World War II."[9]

The 1st Marine Division reported its last peacetime quarterly training period for April–June 1950, noting that 88 percent of its personnel had qualified in basic skills. Field training by all units reflected the new energy instilled in the division by Major General Erskine, perhaps demonstrating that the difficult period of reassembling the division from its Far East odyssey had ended.

Amphibious training received noteworthy emphasis, and Exercise Demon III (noted above) had involved over twenty-five hundred men, with the 5th Marines remaining in the field another four days after its conclusion for regimental exercises that included drilling for "attack on organized positions, pursuit and attack of a withdrawing enemy, defense and resumption of the attack." All of the training included using close air support.[1] The marine corps squadrons based on the Pacific Coast all reported pilots in excess of allowance, although not all were in flight status. The six fighter squadrons reported their pilots well qualified in guns, bombs, rockets, instrument flying, and ground-controlled approach, and in the techniques of air search, rescue, and air support. One fighter squadron lagged overall because it was converting to the new jets, but three others (VMF-214, 312, and 323) recorded twenty-eight, thirty, and twenty of their rated thirty-four pilots as carrier qualified in their F4U-4B Corsairs.[11]

The Headquarters Marine Corps staff probably gave only passing interest to an important letter from the army. The corps had procured several new weapons at or after the end of the war, but with little ammunition provided. Three of these were antitank weapons: 57mm and 75mm recoilless rifles, and the 3.5-inch rocket launcher, an improved "bazooka." A new $35 million program would buy emergency stocks of munitions for these weapons, but only for army requirements. The letter solicited Navy Department needs and funds in order to ensure a share of the program.[12] Unfortunately, the navy acquired very little of this materiel as the summer of 1950 loomed.[13]

Most observers have depicted the postwar years as a period of impoverishment for America's armed services, with spending cuts imposed on general-purpose forces in order to finance the technological panaceas of air power and nuclear weaponry. But any survey of the activities and actions of the marine corps during this period indicates that it had, with much thought and effort, maintained a force capable of most military functions, although not of the scale that war plans required. Nevertheless, the United States retained some conventional fighting power. Marines formed part of that good news, but by no means did they stand alone in that respect.

The Crisis of 1950

War continued in East Asia after World War II, and very shortly after civil war had decided China's fate, was Korea's turn. What remained in doubt at the time, however, was the question of whether the 25 June 1950 North Korean invasion represented a local quarrel or the precursor to World War III, serving as a stratagem to lure Western attention and forces away from what would be the real main effort—the Soviet invasion of Western Europe.

North Korean leader Kim Il Sung had frequently requested support from both China and the Soviet Union for an invasion of South Korea. Soviet dictator Josef Stalin usually insisted that Kim wait until his forces had gained overwhelming military superiority before launching an attack. To that end he approved, in February 1950, the shipment of weapons and equipment to North Korea that enabled the Korean People's Army (KPA) to expand to more than ten divisions by the time of the invasion. Soviet advisors were also provided to assist with planning and training. Finally, Stalin and Mao approved Kim's invasion during talks held in April and May of 1950.

North Korean operational plans for the invasion called for a general advance across the border (38th Parallel), with KPA forces advancing ten–thirteen miles per day to complete the occupation of the peninsula within twenty-two and twenty-seven days.[14]

On the eve of the invasion, the KPA had concentrated along the demarcation line in the strength of eleven infantry divisions reinforced by 120 medium tanks of the 105th Armored Brigade (later redesigned an armored division). A considerable number of the troops had fought in the recent Chinese civil war, and a few had taken part in the Sino-Japanese conflict.[15]

Surprise can confer a great advantage in war, and despite determined resistance by units of the outnumbered and ill-prepared Republic of Korea (ROK) Army, the North Korean onslaught of 25 June 1950 rolled through its objectives, occupying Seoul, the South Korean capital,

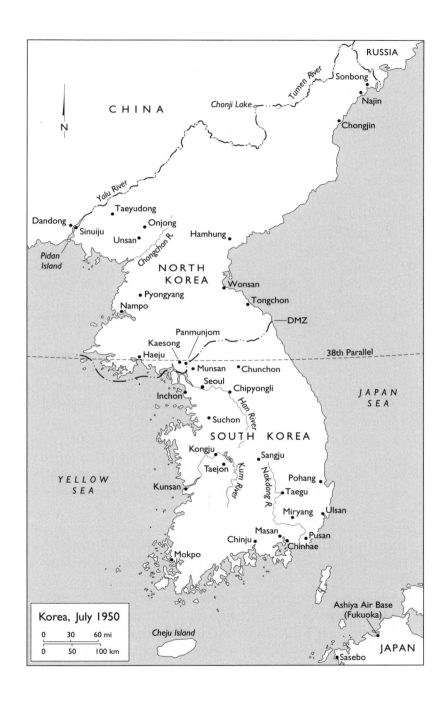

Korea, July 1950

0	30	60 mi
0	50	100 km

13

on 28 June and continuing to drive south with ROK troops fleeing before it. The ROK Army salvaged only two of eight divisions intact from this retreat and only 30 percent of its equipment and 55 percent of its troops remained overall. The disaster seemed complete.[16]

The Western world reacted with shock and surprise to the news from the Koreas, and on the afternoon of 25 June the United Nations Security Council declared a breach of the peace. Calling for a cessation of hostilities and a North Korean withdrawal to the 38th Parallel, the council further required "all Members to render every assistance to the United Nations in the execution of this resolution and to refrain from giving assistance to the North Korean authorities."[17]

That evening, President Truman ordered the commander in chief of Far East Command in Tokyo, General of the Army Douglas MacArthur, to provide munitions and equipment to the Republic of Korea; evacuate American families, civilian and military; and recommend the aid required to save the nation.

As the news went from bad to worse, President Truman authorized the dispatch of combat troops to Korea to secure the seaport and air facilities in the vicinity of Pusan (pop. 948,000) in the southeast corner of the peninsula, and also ordered the air and naval bombardment of North Korea. Interestingly, at this early date no action in the vicinity of Seoul or the Han River by ground troops was considered, only the retention of an enclave on the peninsula.[18]

The initial response by the Joint Chiefs of Staff to MacArthur's reports was to prepare reinforcements for East Asia, as authorized by President Truman on 29 June 1950. Commandant of the Marine Corps General Clifton B. Cates had urged the chief of naval operations to offer a marine corps brigade the day before, but had to wait two days before gaining approval. Cates's briefing included the manpower strength of the Fleet Marine Forces, Pacific (11,853) and Atlantic (15,803), showing that neither one could immediately provide a complete marine division.[19]

Chief of Naval Operations Admiral Forest Sherman cabled his Pacific Fleet commander, Admiral Arthur Radford, on 1 July, asking how soon marines could be embarked. With the prompting of his Fleet Marine Force, Pacific staff, Radford responded overnight that he could ready a battalion in four days and a reinforced regiment (regimental combat team, or RCT) in six days after receipt of orders. The loaded ships would be able to sail in six and ten days respectively from the time of order. Thus, on 2 July Admiral Sherman could confidently issue the following order:

> Make initial preparations to mount out at earliest practicable date one regimental combat team from FMFPac with [an] appropriate marine air unit for tactical air support for duty Western Pacific under operational control CINCFE. Probable such duty will involve combat operations Korea with possibility amphibious employment. Advise OPNAV your plans for this movement when formulated.[20]

After a series of exchanges between Pearl Harbor and Washington commands, Admiral Sherman approved the final deployment plan on 4 July. The regiment would sail in a convoy of three attack transports, two dock landing ships, two attack cargo ships, and a destroyer transport, all capable of executing amphibious landing operations, in company with a troopship and an additional cargo ship administratively carrying the aircraft group's ground echelon and thirty days of supplies. Two escort carriers (small aircraft carriers developed in World War II) would carry the aircraft squadrons of Marine Aircraft Group 33 (MAG-33). Upon sailing, the forces would come under MacArthur's operational control.[21]

While marines scrambled to prepare their forces and the navy marshaled its ships, Lieutenant General Shepherd flew to Tokyo to meet with MacArthur and his staff. On 10 July the two commanders conferred and agreed that the rest of the 1st Marine Division could be made ready for an amphibious landing by 1 September. Shepherd suggested that he draft a dispatch for MacArthur's signature, making the official request to the Joint Chiefs. But Shepherd had already prepared the draft and the message went out that night. Shepherd's motives presaged the two-front nature of the marine corps campaign in the Korean War, facing both the enemy and confronting the dominance of the U.S. Air Force and Army: a marine corps regiment "would probably be attached or integrated into an Army Division thus losing its identity as a Marine organization" and the aviation of the "Marine Air-Ground Team would be assigned to the Far Eastern Air Force Command."[22]

The 1st Provisional Marine Brigade formed on 7 July 1950 under the command of Brigadier General Edward A. Craig, the assistant division commander and senior officer present at Camp Pendleton,

General Erskine having been detailed earlier to a State Department-sponsored mission. Craig's deputy commander, Brigadier General Thomas J. Cushman, also commanded the aviation component, consisting of Marine Aircraft Group 33 with its three fighter squadrons. Marine Observation Squadron 6 (VMO-6) remained under the brigade headquarters organization.

Craig had commanded the brigade in its previous activation (1 June 1947–10 May 1949) when it served as the last marine corps combat headquarters remaining in the Western Pacific Theater, controlling marine forces withdrawing from China. For this expedition, it would deploy in peacetime strength, because the 1st Marine Division had little additional combat power to place into it. The immediate problem centered on the infantry or rifle units. Not only did the three infantry battalions of 5th Marine Regiment have only two of the normal three rifle companies, but also the rifle companies had only two of three required rifle platoons.

Craig requested permission to fill out the understrength rifle platoons on 3 July, but this met resistance. General Shepherd telegraphed on 5 July that he had no desire to further deplete the 1st Marine Division. But on 6 July, General Craig responded to Shepherd, indicating General Cates's approval of the additional platoons authorized by the commandant of the marine corps on 5 July, and stating that the composition and strength of the brigade to be activated on 7 July would total 4,767 officers and men. One can only surmise that Cates had overruled Shepherd, perhaps after consulting his own staff, and had approved the augmentation. This may well be the reason for Shepherd's apparent testiness upon his return from Tokyo on 12 July.[23]

Acting in complete confidence of Cates's backing, Shepherd had apparently denied Craig's repeated requests in order to improve the situation concerning the deployment of the entire 1st Marine Division as quickly as possible to Korea, having just engineered the decision with MacArthur to effect that very deployment. Now, Major General O. P. Smith, arriving on 26 July from Washington to take command of the division, would have even fewer riflemen and no chief of staff, thanks to Craig's "not satisfactory" actions and "unnecessary" requisitions. General Smith seems to have borne no such resentment, for in his own view the marine brigade had sailed with about 32 percent of the division staff, "as was quite proper, including several key members of the staff."[24]

This simple vignette matters relatively little in the history of the brigade, except for the contrary telling given it in the marine corps official history, covered in more detail in the final chapter of this work. This official version bore considerable evidence of Shepherd's hand: "Before leaving [for Tokyo], Shepherd found time to recommend formation of a third platoon for the rifle companies of the 5th Marines, and [the] CNO [chief of naval operations] gave his approval the following day."[25]

Headquarters Marine Corps made many significant contributions to the formation of the brigade in these early days, apart from deciding the issue of the third rifle platoons. Of urgent consideration was the equipping of the brigade with potent antitank (AT) weapons, in view of the effective use of Soviet-made T-34 medium tanks by the North Koreans against South Korean and U.S. Army units. The 2.36-inch rocket launcher, the well-known "bazooka" of World War II fame, was evaluated as completely ineffective against this tank; likewise, the army's M24 light tanks, equipping the divisional tank companies based in Japan, could not slug it out with the Soviet mediums.

On 7 July, MacArthur's command, in cognizance of the threat posed by Soviet armor, informed the Joint Chiefs that the marine corps regimental combat team then loading on the West Coast "should load with it maximum amount of anti-tank material which can be carried without delaying planned estimated time of departure. Strongly recommend 3.5 AT rocket with HEAT ammunition and AT mines as well as other types AT weapons." Unfortunately, no ammunition could be found for the 3.5-inch bazooka, because the army had shipped it directly to Japan as soon receiving it from the manufacturer.[26]

The corps had by then acquired 102 M26 Pershing medium tanks, which had seen limited action in Europe in 1945, and had husbanded them in storage for just such wartime use. This pragmatic economy measure allowed the two active-duty tank battalions to operate a few as training vehicles while still using their M4A3 Shermans, issued in 1944. On 3 July, the 1st Marine Division had requested the issue of enough M26s (plus ammunition for the Pershing's 90mm main gun) to outfit the brigade's tank company. Headquarters ordered the issue of both tanks and ammunition from West Coast depot stocks, and turned immediately to solving ammunition deficiencies. On 11 July, the staff advised that all 90mm ammo would arrive by noon the next day except for smoke (white phosphorous) projectiles.[27]

As noted in an undated memo filed on 5 July summarizing the antitank effort of the staff (principally guided by Lieutenant Colonel Arthur J. Stuart, the marine corps' *eminence gris* of tank warfare), twelve units of fire (a logistics computation for an "average day" in action per gun) for the best 90mm high-velocity antitank ammunition (HVAP) were shipped instead of the eight units of fire requested. This ammunition had tested far superior to the armor of the T-34 tank. The seventeen M26 tanks replaced the existing M4A3 mediums of the brigade's tank company; five additional Pershings would be shipped at a later date. Headquarters furnished a total of eighty 3.5-inch rocket launchers in addition to the older 2.36-inch launchers already in the hands of the troops. Powerful antitank mines, with four times the previous explosive content of the mines then in use, would be airlifted to the division for issue to the brigade. Finally, all antitank ammunition for the 75mm recoilless rifles and the 2.36-inch rocket launchers of the infantry battalions, the armored amphibious tractor 75mm howitzers, and the 105mm howitzers of the artillery battalion were shipped to meet required operational levels.[28]

Like the marine corps, the army was troubled by the North Korean tank threat, and took steps to deal with it. On 11 July, three army tank battalions, based in the United States and outfitted with M26 or M46 tanks (the latter an M26 with an improved engine and transmission package) were ordered to Korea.[29]

The United States was beginning to project a great wave of reinforcement toward Korea, and although the marine brigade would not be the first formation to arrive from the United States nor the first operating the M26 tank, it would make its mark nonetheless.

MacArthur's headquarters resolved the apparent dilemma of the missing 3.5-inch rocket ammunition for the brigade's eighty improved and lethal M20 "super-bazooka" rocket launchers on 13 July, promising a complete issue by Eighth Army upon arrival.[30]

As a final insurance against the tank problem in Korea, the marine corps searched for an effective antitank rifle grenade for immediate issue to the troops. The marine corps had tested the Belgian "Energa" antitank rifle grenade in 1949, and found it more than twice as effective as older munitions in stock. Headquarters executed an emergency acquisition (eleven tons) of the Energa as the 1st Provisional Marine Brigade headed for the Korean War in July 1950. However, half of these were lost when one of the two Douglas R4C transports carrying the shipment crashed at Tinker Air Force Base. The corps bought the next three tons of production and shipped it as well. Happily, very few of these last-ditch defensive weapons proved necessary. The Energa-type grenade continued in marine corps service into the 1970s.[31]

Personnel issues in this phase included the ordering of the first replacement draft to replace expected casualties. The commandant directed on 15 July that 50 officers and 747 enlisted marines and one officer and 14 enlisted navy personnel (medical personnel assigned to marine corps units) be assembled at Marine Barracks, Treasure Island, California for arrival in theater not later than 1 September. Planners accelerated this scheme as combat actions ensued. The brigade sailed at peacetime strength but with personnel having sufficient enlistment time remaining to deploy for a year, leaving considerable turmoil in what remained behind at the West Coast bases of the marine corps. The corps sought to rectify this problem on 12 July by suspending until further notice the normal limits on an individual's length of tour on foreign and sea duty for enlisted personnel. Personnel awaiting transfers mandated by headquarters would still transfer, but personnel not desiring to reenlist or extend enlistments for the deployments would still go out, to be returned "with sufficient time to execute discharges."[32]

First Orders

By this time, however, matters other than the brigade's departure had begun to press on the headquarters staff. On 3 July, the chief of naval operations ordered another marine corps fighter squadron to the carrier USS *Midway* prior to her 10 July departure from Norfolk to the Mediterranean. On 12 July, Admiral Sherman indicated that executive authority under the Second Emergency Increment would soon authorize full peacetime strength for the 1st Marine Division, and the 1st Provisional Marine Brigade. On 19 July, the president authorized the call-up of the marine corps reserve, allowing the commandant to tap its organized units and individual replacements, amounting to some 127,000 marines. The chief of naval operations then sent his warning order on 2 August to prepare to mount out the rest of 1st Marine Division, as well as contingents sufficient to bring the 1st Provisional Marine Brigade to wartime strength and additional fighter squadrons to MacArthur's command during the period 10–15 August.[33]

The first wave of naval reinforcements began to leave the United States in early July. However, tensions remained high with the perceptions that the Korean conflict merely presaged an outbreak of general war, presumably with the Soviet Union. Admiral Sherman urged the greatest speed to his fleet commanders, but initially the Pacific Fleet commanders sailed in complete task groups or increments; and the first sailings from San Diego came only after its channels were swept for mines. Some message traffic included anti-sabotage alerts. Once arrived at Pearl Harbor, some ships proceeded unescorted and others in groups, arriving at Japanese ports beginning 18 July.[34]

In part the need for urgency manifested in the mobilization stage stemmed from MacArthur's zeal for conducting as soon as possible an amphibious counterattack on the west coast of Korea at Inchon. The trick lay in balancing the forces needed to stop the North Korean attack toward Pusan in the southeast while at the same time assembling a strategic reserve needed to land in the enemy's rear with complete naval and air superiority. In a 5 July teletype exchange between Admiral Sherman and Admiral Radford, then in Tokyo, Radford indicated that MacArthur intended to sail on 17 July with the 1st Cavalry Division and land two battalions abreast in an assault at Inchon on July 22. The 1st Provisional Marine Brigade, including its aircraft carried in an administrative dense-loading on board a single escort carrier, could not support this landing and conceivably might have been used for a later assault landing on west coast of Korea north of the 38th parallel.

But such a perilous operation could not be undertaken in the current circumstances, which found the divisions of the U.S. Eighth Army and its South Korean allies continuing to fall back before the North Korean attacks, gathering by mid-July for a defense around the city of Taejon. As the army official historian noted, "It is clear that by the time the 24th Division retreated across the Kum River and prepared to make a stand in front of Taejon there was no complacency over the military situation in Korea in either Eighth Army or the Far East Command. Both were thoroughly alarmed."[35]

Accordingly, the mission of the marine brigade began to change after its departure from the United States. Prior orders had directed it to make port at Sasebo, Japan, for possible use in amphibious operations, but on 25 July MacArthur directed his naval staff to reroute it directly to Pusan, leaving the aviation elements in their intended destination of Kobe port and Itami Air Base in Japan: "Be prepared [to] execute rapid non-tactical debarkation of elements required for conventional ground combat. Units and equipment peculiar to amphibious operations will be retained on board or will be reloaded for shipment [to] Kobe." For the embarked units, confusion mounted. Would the brigade go into the attack or merely cover a withdrawal? This matter would interfere with General Craig's later intention to prepare for immediate combat.[36]

In the Navy sealift carrying the 1st Provisional Marine Brigade, Task Group 53.7 consisted of:

Attack transports: *George Clymer, Henrico, Pickaway*
Attack cargo ships: *Whiteside, Alshain, Achernar*
Landing ships dock: *Gunston Hall, Fort Marion*
Transport: *General A. E. Anderson*
Destroyer transport: *H. A. Buss*[37]

The 1st Provisional Marine Brigade departed San Diego in its navy assault shipping on 12 and 14 July. The two weeks of feverish preparation to date had collected the men in the required numbers and specialties, processing them for overseas deployment and, if any time could be spared, allowing them to familiarize themselves with weapons and equipment. No reservists yet could be mobilized, and the new rifle platoons of necessity came from units external to the 5th Marines, and external to Camp Pendleton if the required men could not be found at that base. Assembling the tank company, so vital for the pending encounter with North Korean armor, proved difficult. Only two of the five M26 tanks of the training platoon of the 1st Tank Battalion remained serviceable for deployment, and fifteen of A Company's tanks came from the Barstow depot, shipped out of the storage lot with many of their critical parts still packed and coated in cosmoline (a thick, sticky oil distillate used for preserving parts in storage). On 7 July, the gunner and loader of each crew fired a few practice shots with their tank's 90mm gun at Camp Pendleton's range. But most of the crewmen spent day and night pierside in San Diego with their tanks, cleaning and scraping and assembling the components, loading ammunition, greasing suspension systems, and finally loading the vehicles on landing craft for movement to their assigned ships.[38]

Much has been written about the apparent fitness and experience of the marines of the 1st Provisional Marine Brigade, and these accounts generally presume that the best of the finest were hand-picked for this initial contingent. But this, in fact, was not the case— nor could it be, given the circumstances of filling out third rifle platoon in each of the six rifle companies of the 5th Marines, and similar shuffling of personnel in other outfits to achieve a proper balance of grade and remaining time-in-service.

Although Shepherd's initial orders had specified a total force not to exceed forty-five hundred men, more than six thousand marines mustered with the brigade for its deployment. The ground element centered on the 5th Marines, and most of the personnel stood in the regiment and the attachments of divisional artillery, tank, engineer, and weapons units that normally formed with a regimental combat team.

Brigade Leaders

In marine corps lore the leadership of the brigade consisted of tough-minded veterans of the Pacific War who led their seasoned charges into battle against a new foe. Such is reflected in the official history versions. For example, in *U.S. Operations in Korea*, authors Lynn Montross and Nicholas Canzona state that "a glance at the NCOs, the platoon leaders and company commanders of the Brigade could only have brought a gleam of pride to the Commandant's battle wise eye. With few exceptions, they were veterans of World War II who could be relied upon to get the best out of their men."[39]

Similarly, John Chapin, writing in *Fire Brigade*, asserts that "90 percent of the brigade's officers had seen combat before on the bloody beaches and in the jungles of the Pacific. This was also the case for two-thirds of the staff noncommissioned officers. Here was a group of leaders well prepared for the rigors of combat."[40]

In fact, a "glance" at the personnel records shows that sergeants and below generally had enlisted no earlier than 1945, almost too late to have participated in any ground action, because the Battle of Okinawa (involving only two of the six marine corps divisions taking part in the Pacific War) ended that June. This was also the case for many staff sergeants. As well, a significant number of officers (apart from most of the pilots) lacked combat experience. Although General Craig and Lieutenant Colonel Murray each wore Navy Crosses awarded

1ST PROVISIONAL MARINE BRIGADE JULY 1950

HEADQUARTERS AND SERVICE BATTALION
1ST PROVISIONAL MARINE BRIGADE

Detachment, 1st Signal Battalion
Detachment, 1st Service Battalion
Detachment, 1st Combat Service Group, FMF
1st Platoon, Reconnaissance Company, 1st Marine Division
1st Platoon, Military Police Company, 1st Marine Division
1st Amphibian Truck Platoon, FMF
Company A, 1st Engineer Battalion
Company A, 1st Motor Transport Battalion
Company A, 1st Ordnance Battalion
Company A, 1st Shore Party Battalion
Company A, 1st Tank Battalion
Company C, 1st Medical Battalion
1st Amphibian Tractor Company, FMF

5TH MARINE REGIMENT

4.2-inch Mortar Company, 1st Weapons Battalion
75mm Recoilless Gun Company, 1st Weapons Battalion
1st Battalion, 11th Marines

The personnel strength of the brigade ground element totaled 281 Marine Corps officers and 4,743 enlisted men, and 37 officers and 153 enlisted of the navy.

MARINE AIRCRAFT GROUP 33

VMF–214: 24 F4U-4B fighter-bombers
VMF–323: 24 F4U-4B fighter-bombers
VMF(N)–513: 12 F4U-5N night fighters
VMO–6: 8 OY observation-liaison airplanes and 4 HO3S-1 helicopters (attached to brigade HQ)

The brigade aviation element included 182 officers and 1,366 men USMC, and 5 officers and 26 USN. The brigade total therefore came to 463/6109 Marine Corps and 42/179 U.S. Navy personnel, considerably more than the usually reported numbers.

Source: Task organization and personnel strength in Smith A-M, 1; Shepherd's personnel ceiling was stated in CG FMFPac 050101ZAug50; RG127/E162/10; some confusion may have resulted from the separation of organizations sent to carriers or Japan. The brigade reported to Eighth Army with an effective in-country (Korea) strength of 4,659; U.S. Eighth Army, Korea (hereafter EUSAK) personnel report (time) 1800, 6Aug50, RG407/E429/1092.

for exploits recorded during the Marianas Campaign, the three infantry battalion commanders had missed out on the fighting. Most captains had fought in the previous war, but the lieutenants had not, except for those commissioned from the ranks. The aircraft group commander had commanded transport groups in California and the South Pacific. His immediate superior, the deputy brigade commander, had been first the chief of staff, Marine Corps Air Wings, Pacific (an administrative organization), and had then commanded air defenses in the Marianas after they were secured, subsequently returning to the United States in April 1945.

How this "combat veterans" legend took shape remains unknown, and it added little to the record of the brigade; the performance of the well-trained but mostly inexperienced officers and enlisted men only reflected even more credit upon marine corps culture.[41]

Brigadier General Edward A. Craig (1896–1994), as mentioned above, was the exception that proved the rule. Craig had grown up on army posts as the son of an officer. At the time of America's entry into World War I, he was attending St. John's Military Academy in Denfield, Wisconsin. Rather than wait another year for his twenty-first birthday, he telegrammed his father, "I'm entering the Marine Corps. I have a chance for a commission." The reply came quickly, "Do not join the U.S. Marines under any circumstances. A terrible bunch of drunks and bums. Father"[42]

Craig joined the marines anyway, but missed assignment to France; instead the young officer instead cut his teeth on duty in the Caribbean, the Philippines, and at sea. Rising to the rank of captain, Craig served as aide-de-camp to marine corps icon and commandant, Major General John A. Lejeune, during what turned out to be the great man's final three years in uniform. Assignments in Nicaragua, at Quantico, and at Norfolk on the Atlantic Fleet Staff followed. During World War II, he reported to then-Colonel Shepherd as executive officer and in July 1943 succeeded him as commander of the 9th Marines, leading that regiment in the assaults on Bougainville and Guam. He earned the Navy Cross for his actions on Guam, and subsequently served as the V Amphibious Corps operations officer in the Battle for Iwo Jima. Promoted to brigadier general after the war, he commanded the 1st Provisional Marine Brigade in China and Guam before reporting to 1st Marine Division as its assistant commander.

Brigadier General Thomas J. Cushman (1895–1972) served as Craig's titular deputy, but functioned more as an aviation component commander for the brigade. Cushman graduated from the University of Washington and enlisted in the Corps in 1917. Commissioned on 22 October 1918, he received his naval aviator designation after completing flight training in July 1919. Although not one of the corps' aviation pioneers, he nevertheless distinguished himself in the early years of the branch, with overseas tours in Guam, Nicaragua, and Haiti. Completing aeronautical engineering courses in the early 1930s, he commanded Observation Squadron 8 in 1936 for a year, then spent another year commanding Marine Fighting Squadron 2 before returning to duties commanding bases on the East Coast in 1939. His real experience of war began only in 1944, as a temporary brigadier general and deputy commander of the 4th Marine Base Air Wing for five months followed by six months as commander of the air defenses of the Marianas. In April 1945, he returned to the United States to spend the next two years in multiple assignments as an air base commander. In 1947 he was promoted to the permanent grade of brigadier general and assigned as chief of staff for Aircraft, Fleet Marine Force Pacific, assuming command of that entity on 5 February 1948.

Colonel Allen C. Koonce (1905–1972) graduated from the Naval Academy in 1927 and completed flight training in 1930. During World War II, from 1943 through 1945, he commanded air transport groups in the South Pacific. Afterward, Koonce commanded yet another transport unit before joining the staff of Aircraft, Fleet Marine Force, Pacific, in 1948. At the time of the Korean crisis, Colonel Koonce had assumed duties as chief of staff, 1st Marine Aircraft Wing, serving in that post for a few months before taking command of Marine Aircraft Group 33. Frank G. Dailey, a highly experienced World War II fighter pilot, replaced him on 23 August 1950.[43]

In stark contrast to their superiors, the fighter squadron commanders, all lieutenant colonels, had considerable experience in aerial combat. J. Hunter Reinburg (1918–1997), commanding the night fighters, was an ace (seven victories, four while flying the F4U Corsair). Arnold A. Lund (1919–1966) flew fighters in combat in the Marshalls, while Walter Lischeid (1918–1950), a latecomer to aviation in 1943 as a major, took command of VMF-323 in early 1945. Under his command the squadron took part in the Okinawa campaign, claiming twenty-nine Japanese aircraft before the end of the war.[44]

Lieutenant Colonel Raymond L. Murray (1913–2004) took command of the 5th Marines in June after the departure of Colonel Krulak for his new post in Hawaii as G-3 (operations chief of staff) to General Shepherd. Murray had received his commission in the marine corps in 1935 after graduating from Texas A&M University. First posted to San Diego with the 6th Marines, he served two years in China with its 2nd Battalion and the Peking Guard detachment. Returning to the United States in early 1941, he sailed with the 6th Marines in May of that year for occupation duty in Iceland. As commanding officer of the 2nd Battalion, he later fought at Guadalcanal, Tarawa, and Saipan, receiving serious wounds in the latter assault, where he also earned the Navy Cross, which he added to his two Silver Star medals from the previous island battles. After convalescing in the U.S, he held postwar student, academic, and staff assignments, including inspector of Marine Garrison Forces, Pacific. He reported to the 1st Marine Division in January 1949.

In contrast to the situation in the aircraft group, the 5th Marines had a combat experienced commanding officer overseeing three infantry battalion commanders possessing no infantry experience whatsoever from World War II. George W. Newton (1915–1993) had been a company commander in the Peking Guard, which was forced to surrender in December 1941; like every other marine in that detachment, he spent the entire war in Japanese prison camps. Harold S. Roise (1916–1991) experienced the Pearl Harbor attack on board the battleship USS *Maryland*, and subsequently served on the more modern battleship USS *Alabama* in the Atlantic and Pacific. Robert D. Taplett (1918–2005) served on the heavy cruiser USS *Salt Lake City* through the end of the war. Thus, each of the three infantry battalion commanders not only lacked combat infantry experience, but also had never commanded a marine corps rifle company. One assumes that the marine corps assigned them to command in order to catch up professionally with their peers. The Korean War would immediately test this measure.[45]

Commanding the brigade's artillery battalion (1st Battalion, 11th Marines), Lieutenant Colonel Ransom M. Wood (1916–2005) had begun his artillery service in 1941 as a battery commander with 5th Defense Battalion after an initial tour at sea. After the war began, he joined the 2nd Defense Battalion in Hawaii before transferring, in April 1942, to the 8th Defense Battalion in the Samoan Defense Area.

In April 1944 he became executive officer of the 5th 155mm Howitzer Battalion (V Amphibious Corps artillery) and took part in combat operations on Saipan and Leyte before returning to the United States in March 1945. Thus, during the war Wood had compiled an impressive record as artillery officer–but, crucially for the battles to come, he had never served with *direct support* artillery units such as the 1/11.

Some of the brigade's 1950 rifle company commanders were, like Wood, handicapped in their assignments by a lack of relevant experience. A random sampling of their World War II records reveals that several of these men, far from being the "seasoned combat veterans" of marine corps lore who had seen heavy action on the "bloody beaches and in the jungles" of Pacific War campaigns, were in fact virtual novices at their trade. For example, Robert D. Bone was commissioned in May 1944 and served on the USS *Monterrey*. Samuel Jaskilka completed training in 1943 and served on the USS *Princeton*, returning to instructor duty in the United States after that ship was sunk in the Battle of Leyte Gulf. Joseph C. Fegan, Jr., commissioned in 1942, served as an artillery officer in the 4th Marine Division, seeing action on Roi-Namur, Saipan, Tinian, and Iwo Jima, and receiving the Silver Star for his performance on Saipan. He continued to serve as an artilleryman until joining the 5th Marines in 1949, when he became an assistant operations officer and then rifle company commander in the regiment's 3rd Battalion.[46]

In the end, the brigade sailed forth with its main advantage being the marine corps' institutional strengths and culture. Marines expect to be "first to fight." In times of crisis, they provide a stabilizing influence or an on-the-scene initial response with a balanced air-ground combat capability. They arrive combat-equipped and fully ready for action. Marines train hard, fight to win, and intend to survive in combat. As in the Pacific War, so in the Korean War: the idea of failure or letting down one's brother marines was simply unthinkable, and would inspire extraordinary feats of exertion and courage.

PREPARING FOR WAR

Although probably no different in intensity than that of their army counterparts, the hurried activities of U.S. Marines to assemble and deploy a complete brigade to Korea required much discipline and flexibility and should not be neglected in assessing its performance. The shortages in men and materiel required much improvisation, and the need to load ships quickly demanded great energy and perseverance. Above all, there was little firm knowledge of what the brigade would be required to do in Korea, a circumstance that required the marines to prepare for practically any eventuality. Moreover, the onset of the Korean War made great demands on military transportation systems, none of which had been maintained in any strength since 1945.

While the men of the 5th Marines and other brigade troops labored in San Diego to load their ships in roughly four days before sailing, the aviation echelon, built around Marine Aircraft Group 33, executed its own load-out from the Marine Corps Air Station at El Toro to the nearby port of Long Beach and finally to the aircraft carrier pier at San Diego's North Island Naval Air Station. To the casual observer, it may have seemed that the aviation units suffered from fewer equipment and readiness issues than their ground brethren, but it turned out that many of the group's required ground support personnel lacked time remaining in their enlistments to deploy; many shortages had to be filled with men not in the required grade or specialty. From 7 through 13 July, some 250 men joined the aircraft group, many without orders and record books. Two of the three fighter squadrons designated for the deployment came from Marine Aircraft Group 12, but "MAG-33" had just completed maneuvers with the division and was considered more ready for the support role with the brigade. It also took other 1st Marine Aircraft Wing organizations such as the observation squadron (VMO-6), the air control squadron (MTACS-2), and the ground control intercept squadron (MGCIS-1). On 14 August, a helicopter detachment from the East Coast experimental helicopter squadron HMX-1 caught up with the group in the nick of time and was attached to VMO-6.[47]

Marines today have sometimes mistaken the brigade's organization as an early example of the current Marine Corps Air-Ground Task Force (MAGTF), which combined aviation and ground units as a matter of course. Nothing could be farther from the truth in July 1950. The brigade headquarters had no air-ground command and control element, and Brigadier General Cushman from the beginning acted somewhat independently, taking the superior title of Commander, Forward Echelon, 1st Marine Aircraft Wing (MAW). Apart from handling affairs of the rear echelon in Japan for the 1st Marine

Provisional Brigade and coordinating the required air support to the ground combat units, it seems clear that he was uninvolved in brigade matters. Relatedly, it will be seen that the aviation echelon operated virtually as a separate supporting organization, which also worked to prepare for the reception on 5 September of its parent 1st Marine Aircraft Wing in Japan. The aviation echelon also brought its own logistics organization, a necessity given that it could hardly have depended upon the slender logistics support echelon of the brigade.

While the aircraft and specialized support equipment of the group crowded on board the escort carrier USS *Badoeng Strait* at the San Diego carrier pier, most personnel and supplies boarded the troopship *General A. B. Anderson* and the cargo ship USS *Achernar* at Long Beach. These vessels departed on 14 July and caught up with the amphibious assault ships of the rest of the brigade to sail in company with them for Japan. The densely packed flight and hangar decks of the escort carrier prohibited flight operations, so both echelons of the brigade faced relative inactivity during the Pacific crossing. The troops received lectures on Korea and what was known of the enemy, and pored over their weapons and relevant tactical and technical manuals. Many squads, teams, and crews had been mixed or thrown together for the first time, and the almost three-week crossing provided an essential basis for later cohesion among brigade units.

The eighty aircraft embarked on the escort carrier for ferrying consisted of fifty-six F4U-4 fighters (eight as navy spares), twelve F4U-5N night fighters, two F4U-5P photo reconnaissance planes, six HO3S-1 helicopters, and eight TOY-3 observation and spotting aircraft (four as marine corps spares). With the exception of the helicopters, these machines had all proven themselves in years of operation and could be capably maintained from lavish stores of parts in the supply system. Even in the case of the more novel HO3S-1, use of this helicopter in naval aviation was well established by 1950.[48]

The ground weapons and equipment also posed few problems of reliability and repair parts supply. The rifles, machine guns, radios, trucks, and artillery pieces operated by the men remained familiar issue items well proven in World War II. The exceptions that now came into marine hands included several key weapons introduced to the marine corps after 1945: the M26 tank, the M30 4.2-inch heavy mortar, the M20 3.5-inch antitank rocket launcher, and the M20 75mm recoilless rifle. Their novelty caused many classes to be held on board the ships as tank and weapons crews studied the manuals. The shortage of training ammunition and time before embarkation meant that marines remained unfamiliar with these items until the brigade entered combat. In the case of the antitank rocket launchers, or "bazookas," it is likely that most men had only practiced on the older M9 or M18 2.36-inch weapons, which had different sights but were employed the same way. However, the new tank, mortar, and recoilless rifle bore much less resemblance to the earlier weapons they had replaced.

As the ships slipped over the horizon from the coast of California and the embarked units settled into shipboard routines for the voyage, new problems cropped up almost immediately. On board the dock landing ship *Fort Marion*, the men of A Company, 1st Tank Battalion lined up on the mess deck for lunch on 13 July. One sergeant tank commander strolled the dry-dock wing walls extending aft and casually scanned the fourteen M26 tanks parked and tied down on the well deck. To his disbelief, seawater lapped at the tanks' fenders. Rushing to his marines, he sounded the alarm. By the time the ships' company had manned the valve controls and properly re-ballasted the ship, four to five feet of salt water had filled the dock well. Five of the fourteen tanks were immersed to their turret rings, their interiors flooded. Damage to wiring disabled several vehicles and it looked for a while that the ship would have to return to California. Long hours of work by crews and maintenance personnel, however, restored all but one of the tanks to combat readiness when offloaded. What could not be compensated for was the loss of three hundred rounds of precious 90mm high-velocity armor piercing ammunition, which had to be jettisoned as water-soaked.[49]

The next day, the attack transport *Henrico* blew a steam condenser and diverted to San Francisco for main propulsion repairs, eventually rejoining the squadron just as it arrived at Pusan. Because the *Henrico* carried the 5th Marines headquarters and the regiment's 1st Battalion, this incident posed another serious threat to the brigade's mission, now barely into the transit phase! The 5th Marines staff transferred to another transport for the rest of the trip.

Once the ships departed the United States, Brigadier General Craig reported to the senior commanders in the Far East and later took a look at his next battlefield. En route, he overflew his last one—Iwo

Jima—on 18 July. It is possible that he hoped that his next fight would prove less taxing. Joining Craig were General Cushman and fourteen other key brigade and aviation staff members. After conferring with Admiral Turner Joy (commander of U.S. Naval Forces Far East) and MacArthur's staff, he and Cushman called on MacArthur himself. Craig listened to MacArthur's typical magisterial monologue before requesting that his aviation echelon be kept under brigade control and not taken over by the "Air Corps" except for emergencies. He noted that the infantry and artillery had not been filled to wartime strength and that air support remained essential. MacArthur agreed and also ordered his staff to request that all future marine corps reinforcements to the theater arrive at wartime strength. Craig's conversations the next day (20 July) with Lieutenant General George Stratemeyer, commander of the Far East Air Forces, confirmed the operational status of marine corps aviation for the moment.[50]

At that point, MacArthur was still contemplating amphibious operations and told Craig that the brigade would likely wait in Japan for the arrival of the 1st Marine Division. By 23 July, Craig and Cushman completed plans to billet the ground troops of the brigade and eventually the division in the Kyoto area and base all aviation at Itami Air Base, with nearby training areas taken over from the army. But while en route to establish his headquarters in Kyoto on 25 July, Craig was recalled to MacArthur's headquarters and received new orders: with the situation deteriorating precipitously on the peninsula, he was to land the brigade at the port of Pusan, Korea, instead of the intended ports in Japan.

Craig flew to Taegu and reported to General Walker on the afternoon of 26 July. Using a liaison plane furnished by Walker, he toured Pusan the next day, checked its docks and railhead, and conferred with the army port commander. He then returned to Taegu, flying over fields near Masan village where the brigade would eventually assemble. He also made a quick reconnaissance of the Pusan Perimeter lines just then being occupied by the Eighth Army. Craig moved his advance party to Pusan on the 30 July and awaited the arrival of his embarked units.

Despite his best intentions the brigade would split up, as no suitable airfields existed within the Pusan Perimeter. Admiral Joy ordered the ships carrying the aviation elements to offload at Kobe and General

Cushman's staff established his 1st Marine Aircraft Wing (Forward) headquarters and Marine Aircraft Group 33 at Itami. From there, the two fighter squadrons would transfer to escort carriers for further operations afloat and the night fighters would fly under Fifth Air Force orders from Japan. Only an air control unit and the observation squadron would join the brigade in Korea.

2

FIRST FORTNIGHT IN KOREA

Brigadier General Edward A. Craig, USMC, stood a lonely vigil at the port of Pusan on 1 August, lacking any means of communicating with his brigade except via Eighth Army operators and equipment and without his principal commanders. In his field notebook he noted that his brigade would probably be committed on the Eighth Army left flank after landing at Pusan. After a day spent with his skeleton staff planning along these lines, he issued his Brigade Operation Order 3–50 ordering units to prepare for immediate combat operations. Nothing more could be done for the moment, but he remained troubled, remarking tersely in his field notebook that the "absence of [the] third rifle company in each battalion will be critical but people who made [the] decision to deny me this will be in a safe place, and the cost will be in lives—not theirs."[1]

The operations order that Craig drafted directed the 5th Marines to prepare for immediate debarkation at Pusan fully ready for combat operations. He intended that the ships disgorge their men and equipment as fully armed and equipped units, carrying a day's allowance of ammunition, with the rest of the supplies to follow them once they marched off the pier to their assembly area. All the loading in California had been administrative in nature, counting upon the use of ports in Japan for any rapid reconfiguration for new missions. Craig knew that he was making an extreme demand upon his commanders, one likely to produce a flurry of unorthodox activities on board the ships. Most likely, he trusted in their leadership and training to make it happen. However, his orders either never left the Eighth Army communications center or were never received by the ship carrying Lieutenant Colonel Murray and his staff. The ships carrying the brigade steered for Pusan and Sasebo, and the marines knew little of what awaited them upon arrival.

Pressure from all sides mounted for every U.N. unit in Korea. For the Eighth Army a crucial test had already arrived and been passed. After the fall of the Kum River line and Taejon (20 July), U.N. forces struggled to preserve a foothold around Pusan until reinforcements arrived to stabilize the situation. The U.N. forces withdrew into their best defensive position, based upon the Naktong River line, at the end of July, with three American divisions in place from the former Japan garrison. The surviving and reorganizing ROK Corps held the northern rim of the perimeter. General Walker and his commanders quite ruthlessly sacrificed green and untried units and shipments of replacements to block the last attempts by the North Koreans to break through the Pusan Perimeter in the north, between Taegu and the sea, or to turn the army's flank to the south, where no major units of either side had been positioned to date. In particular, the thrust by the KPA's 6th Division's toward Masan in the south had been stopped and that division reduced to half strength. Up to that point, the 6th Division had experienced an easy campaign, occupying areas of southwest Korea in a vast turning movement against little if any opposition. Amid the cumulative bloodletting, U.N. forces succeeded for the first time in stopping the North Koreans at the very point that key U.N. reinforcements were about to arrive.[2]

The military reputation of Walton Walker and the Eighth Army has suffered excessively because of later events. Walker's death at the time that Chinese forces routed the Eighth Army in late 1950 compromised most views of his earlier performance. One can easily propose an alternate view of this officer, as well as the American and ROK actions early in the war, and the defense of the Pusan Perimeter. The American and ROK forces performed some of the most difficult military operations of the entire war in July 1950, withdrawing hundreds of miles while badly outnumbered and under serious pressure that included enemy air attacks, yet standing firm in several key positions in order to buy time for reinforcements to accumulate. In the end, Walker and the Eighth Army saved themselves and the vital port of

Pusan, through which the U.N. reinforcements of August could arrive. This event shifted the numerical advantage and eventually reversed the course of the war.

In particular, the North Korean operational deployment around the left flank of the Eighth Army in late July showed the excellence of its commanders and the resilience of its troops. Of all the North Korean moves following the seizure of Seoul, this stroke held the best chances for final victory for Kim's army. At the very moment that American and ROK forces were setting up a strong defense line against which the KPA would break, the Eighth Army had to pull major units out of its center front and move them into a fluid situation in the southwest, where the enemy could move with alacrity to outflank the new Pusan Perimeter and seize the port of Pusan itself with a single thrust.

The Eighth Army never faced impending defeat so critically as in the few days of late July and early August 1950.[3]

Despite the battering that the Eighth Army had received at the hands of the North Koreans, its commander held no doubts as to his future objectives. General Walker, then sixty-one years old, drew on the experiences of service in the two world wars and especially his command of the XX Corps, Third Army, in the European Theater of Operations in 1944–45. One of Lieutenant General George S. Patton's favorite generals in Northwest Europe Campaign, Walker had also gained the attention of the Allied supreme commander, General Eisenhower, who rated him eighteenth of all army generals in Europe. "Top flight Corps C.G., fighter, cool, he has consistently led his corps with an exemplary boldness, and success. He is a fighter in every sense of the word, whether in pursuit or in more difficult conditions of attack against a fortified position."

Thus, Walker spoke from considerable experience when he ordered: "Daily counterattacks will be made by all units. . . . Commanders will take immediate and aggressive action to insure that these and previous instructions to this effect are carried out without delay. Counterattack is a decisive element of the defense."[4]

Already, Walker contemplated taking the offensive, if only to distract enemy forces from their continuing pressure against the northern part of the Pusan Perimeter, especially the heavily engaged "eastern corridor" from Taegu to the sea near the small port of Pohang.

On 4 August, his plans section delivered a staff study that would ineluctably involve the 1st Provisional Marine Brigade. Although noting that the most desirable date for assuming the offensive would be 15–20 August, the planners estimated that this option would give the enemy too much time to rest, reorganize, and recover from its offensive campaign. The recent movement of the U.S. Army's 25th Infantry Division to Masan in order to finally establish a defensive line in the southwest quadrant of the Pusan Perimeter offered an earlier possibility. The army's newly arrived 5th Regimental Combat Team (hereafter, RCT 5, not to be confused with the 5th Marines) and the 1st Provisional Marine Brigade, when added to the 25th Division, constituted "a sufficient force at hand to attack between the 5th and 10th of August." Walker immediately grasped this opportunity to throw his enemy off balance for the first time in the war.[5]

The arrival of the long-awaited reinforcements from the United States made all the difference to Walker's conduct of the battle for Pusan. No longer would the green units from Japan garrisons and replacement levies flown in from the continental United States be bled white to bolster the U.N. positions. Fresh and well-equipped units began to unload at Pusan on 31 July, a port already humming with activity handling supplies and replacements. The first two army regiments had arrived. Unbeknownst to most of the marines, whose mission had been switched from amphibious operations to reinforcing the Pusan Perimeter, several other "fire brigade" type units arrived and began to take part in operations along the entire line. Marine corps lore has held for decades that the 1st Provisional Marine Brigade repeatedly saved the army in the Pusan Perimeter. In order to give proper credit to the brigade for its evident contributions, however, some recognition of the overall situation becomes necessary.

At about the same time that RCT 5 arrived from Hawaii, the first group of reinforcements from the United States also debarked in Korea. This was not the 1st Provisional Marine Brigade, as is often reported in marine corps literature, but rather the army's 9th Regimental Combat Team (RCT 9) from Fort Lewis, Washington. The leading element of the 2nd Infantry Division, RCT 9 sailed on faster troop transports from the United States starting on 17 July. Upon landing at Pusan, it moved to Kyongsan, ten miles southeast of Taegu, and was placed in army reserve. On 8 August, it entered the battle zone at Yongsan, behind the 34th Regimental Combat Team of 24th Infantry Division

(RCT 34). Its artillery began conducting fire missions on 6 August. At the same time, RCT 9 spawned Task Force Bradley, comprising the 3rd Battalion, 9th Infantry; an artillery battery; and the regimental tank company, equipped with M26 tanks. This task force, under the assistant division commander, served as yet another rapid reinforcement unit, sent farther north to the sector of the 1st Cavalry Division.[6]

On 2 August, the ships carrying the 5th Marines finally entered Pusan's harbor, arriving pierside between 1900–2130. Standing at the quay, General Craig observed the troops casually leaning on the railings of the ships, noticeably not wearing their combat gear and not ready to disembark. Spotting his chief of staff, Colonel Edward Snedeker, on the near bridge wing of the transport USS *George Clymer*, he called out, "Did you receive my order?" Snedeker replied that they had not. No extant documents record Craig's response, but it should come as no surprise that an immediate commander's conference ensued on board the *Clymer*.[7]

Unloading and Organizing for Combat

Marines arriving at Pusan feared the worsening situation they had monitored from reports received during their Pacific crossing and wondered openly if they would simply serve to guard a U.N. evacuation at Pusan—a Korean Dunkirk, so to speak. Robert Taplett, commanding the 3rd Battalion, 5th Marines, left the conference with General Craig on USS *George Clymer* that 2 August evening "convinced that our superiors above brigade level thought that the end was near, and we were soon to participate in a massive evacuation from the Korean peninsula." In reality, the situation had already transformed drastically. Although considerable heavy fighting lay ahead, the Eighth Army had achieved much progress.[8]

The more than four thousand officers and men of the 1st Provisional Marine Brigade worked steadily through the night to unload their shipping and then began their movement around 0600 on 3 August to their assembly area (all times local). Eighth Army orders identified this as Changwon, east of Masan in the rear of the 25th Infantry Division. The army had kept its word to support the brigade, immediately providing the debarking marines with vehicles, transportation units, and critical ammunition (notably, 3.5-inch rocket launcher and 90mm HVAP tank munitions). General Craig later remarked that he requested an extra truck company upon the brigade's arrival plus another one for temporary duty in order to execute the moves ordered in the Pusan perimeter at that time. "The army was very good about this," he later wrote, "and they not only furnished the truck companies, but they furnished many communications jeeps and other jeeps for our reconnaissance company . . . and the army service command at Pusan gave us everything we could possibly want in the way of equipment. They were very cooperative."[9]

As the U.N. forces took up positions in the Pusan Perimeter after successfully conducting a fighting withdrawal across the Naktong River, the North Koreans pressed in for the kill. Their military victory would depend upon defeating the Pusan Perimeter defenders before the known U.N. reinforcements arrived. No exertion could be spared, and to contemporary military and press observers, it appeared that the North Korean forces continued to dominate the peninsula.

In point of fact, however, the easy times had passed for the North Korean forces. No longer would they outnumber their opponents on the ground; and the airspace over the peninsula had become completely unfriendly for their aircraft. Their infantry divisions had had little if any respite during the campaign thus far, and they had suffered considerable losses that were becoming increasingly difficult to replace. Their next moves would prove vital to maintaining their momentum. Focusing on the northwest corner of the Pusan Perimeter against Taegu, and in the southwest against Masan, the North Korean 3rd and 6th Infantry Divisions, respectively, attacked along routes that seemed most promising for breaking through the U.N. positions.

The Eighth Army recorded "heavy" enemy pressure on 30 July in these sectors against the 1st Cavalry and 25th Infantry Divisions. Similar pressure also continued against the ROK divisions covering the perimeter's northern sectors. The sole infantry regiment then in army reserve, the 27th Infantry (yet another "fire brigade"), reinforced the 25th Infantry Division and took its position in the lines in the southwest, with the Yellow Sea on its left flank.[10]

The Fifth Air Force established its domination over the peninsula by mid-July, flying up to four hundred sorties per day and completing some eighty-six hundred sorties by the end of July. Fully 50 percent of these sorties consisted of the air force version of close support for ground troops; most of the rest (about 2,550 sorties) entailed "battlefield interdiction," an official term for the ruthless hammering of enemy supply lines. The Far East Air Forces (FEAF) received the first reinforcing fighter aircraft from the U.S. on July 23, and by month's end disposed of almost 900 F-80 jet and F-51 piston-engine fighters, although only 525 were manned and ready for operations.[11]

Fortunately for the forces defending the Pusan Perimeter, the American military's superior logistics capabilities, which had contributed greatly to the Allied victory in the previous war, had not disappeared in the postwar period. These capabilities were now brought fully into play, and the positive effect on U.N. operations was nearly instantaneous. July witnessed a total of 309,314 tons of military supplies and equipment flowing into Pusan, with 230 ships arriving in the second half of the month alone. Ulsan and Suyong served as subsidiary ports, handling ammunition and petroleum mainly over the beaches; and airlift responded to reduce critical shortfalls in the days before sufficient ground transportation could be marshaled. The scheduling of special trains in Japan and ferries across the Sea of Japan resulted in a sea-land supply operation reminiscent of the "Red Ball Express" truck columns that had supplied the rapidly advancing Allied forces in Northwest Europe in the summer of 1944. Korean train lines came under army control and coordination, with daily service from Pusan to the Masan, Taegu, and Pohang termini, using 431 miles of track.[12]

But the most significant development concerning the battle for Pusan was the growing strength of U.N. forces. Parity with the enemy was achieved around 22 July, superiority by the end of August, with some ninety-thousand U.N. troops facing off against approximately seventy-two thousand North Koreans. The U.N. army would continue to grow and retain superiority in numbers until the massive Chinese intervention later in the year. But even before July 1950 the North Koreans at no point possessed the four-to-one advantage commonly cited in contemporary media accounts of the campaign.[13]

But gaining numerical superiority did not resolve lingering problems in command, control, and coordination among the rather disparate elements of the Eighth Army and other U.N. forces. For several weeks, the damage sustained in the previous operational phase would become evident in the form of misunderstood orders and the failure of many units to carry out their tasks. At the same time the North Koreans continued offensive operations, hammering at the perimeter in a desperate bid to break the U.N. lines before the tide turned overwhelmingly

OPPOSING FORCES, KOREA, AUGUST 1950

Korean People's Army (North Korea) 1 August 1950, based on intelligence estimates as 69,100:

Unit Strength

1st Division	5,000
2nd Division	7,500
3rd Division	6,000
4th Division	7,000
5th Division	6,000
6th Division	3,600
8th Division	8,000
2th Division	6,000
13th Division	9,500
15th Division	5,000
105th Armored Division (-)	3,000 (40 tanks)
83rd/105th Motorized Regiment	1,000
766th Infantry Regiment	1,500

MacArthur's command reported American and ROK (South Korean) strength on 4 August 1950 as 141,808:

U.S. Total	59,238
Total Army	50,367
Eighth Army staff	2,933
Korea Military Assistance Group	452
1st Cavalry Division	10,276
2nd Infantry Division	4,922
24th Infantry Division	14,540
25th Infantry Division	12,073
Pusan Base	5,171
1st Provisional Marine Brigade	4,713
FEAF (Korea)	4,051
Other	107
ROK Army (estimated)	82,570

against them. Thus the marine brigade found itself wading into a morass of uncertain operational conditions and repeated surprises at the hands of friend and foe alike.

The brigade began to move out of Pusan as ordered at 0600 the next day, 3 August. With the 1st Battalion, 5th Marines traveling in trucks to the assembly area as an advance guard, the rest of the battalions, tanks, and other equipment (except for two-and-a-half-ton trucks and smaller) boarded Korean trains, which moved sluggishly amid clouds of steam and dense coal smoke to Changwon. Elements of the brigade support echelon either moved with the 5th Marines or remained in Pusan. By 2100, with the arrival of the tanks, the brigade had assembled ashore and in combat order.

Those first days spent in reserve at Masan proved vital to beginning the growth of cohesion in a force that had never worked together and had received many newly assigned personnel. The rumors of enemy movement or infiltration nearby caused a spate of nervous firing through the first night before anxious leaders could regain control. Routine security patrols and gun drills also served to shake out the loose ends of small-unit leadership. The tankers fired their own vehicular weapons to align their sights, most M26 crewmen doing this for the first time with their 90mm cannon. On that first day in the assembly area, the tanks had remained loaded on flatcars, awaiting final deployment orders. The tankers therefore took the novel approach of firing from the flatcars into a nearby hillside to verify their accurate sighting of the 90mm guns. Aerial reconnaissance took on a new significance for unit leaders, thanks to the use of the brigade helicopter detachment. It would take some time to become oriented to the unfamiliar terrain of Korea, with the lack of good maps handicapping the process.[14]

Having yet to engage the North Koreans in combat, the marines found themselves battling equally relentless (if less deadly) foes in the form of Korea's inhospitable terrain and climate. Although a peninsular country almost totally surrounded by the sea, South Korea nevertheless has a continental climate. Summers are hot and humid and in places such as the southeast, semi-tropical. In August, the zone running from Taegu south to the delta of the Naktong River (inclusive of most of the U.N. occupied Pusan Perimeter) remains the hottest place in the two Koreas, at times reaching over 100 degrees Fahrenheit. In late summer, typhoons may bring heavy showers, storms, and flooding along the southern and eastern coasts.

The Korean peninsula has rugged, mountainous terrain, with barely one-fifth of its surface in lowlands or plains. Few of the mountains are high compared to those of other Asian countries, but they are so extensive that there are few places in South Korea where mountains cannot be seen. Visitors new to South Korea see a land resembling a violently stirred sea, because of the large number of successive mountain ranges that crisscross the peninsula. Centuries of deforestation have denuded the landscape, although wooded areas can still be found in the most remote areas. The disappearance of the forests has been a major cause of soil erosion and flooding. Moving away from the much cooler and pleasant coastal enclave of Pusan, the marines entered a region of parallel mountain ranges formed of ancient granite and shale. These mountains had weathered over the ages into sharp or conical peaks and ridges and are rarely more than thirty-three hundred feet (one thousand meters) high.[15]

MAKING PORT IN JAPAN

The offloading of the brigade's aviation units began on 31 July. Upon arrival at Kobe, the escort carrier USS *Badoeng Strait* launched its tactical aircraft at sea by steaming offshore on two days (1–2 August), because of port restrictions. The carrier also offloaded the light OY aircraft and helicopters onto the pier at Kobe, and they flew directly to Itami, the air base designated for the 1st Brigade's use. From Itami, the OYs and helicopters flew on 2 August to Pusan, while the VMO-6 ground echelon and air control personnel moved by Japanese-crewed tank landing ships (LST) to the port and principal Korean naval base of Chinhae, where that squadron began operations with the brigade starting 5 August. The F4U pilots practiced carrier landings at Itami for one to three days before flying to their carriers, because the dense pack of aircraft ferried on the carrier had not permitted any flight operations at sea during the crossing.

The navy designated *Badoeng Strait* and her sister ship, the USS *Sicily*, to carry the two day fighter squadrons for combat operations. After loading equipment and personnel in port, the carriers sortied. Because the *Sicily* had been used for ferry duties in the Far East, the marine aircraft group supply services had to provide a complete F4U spares package for the carrier, her own requisite "Section B" package not arriving from navy sources in the U.S. until September. The night fighter squadron, VMF(N)-513, reported to Fifth Air Force control and staged its operations from Itazuke Air Base, and was therefore effectively lost to the brigade for the rest of the campaign.[16]

Spares and ordnance remained scarce during the first month of operations. The navy initially could not provide the ordnance requirement, estimated as 1,960 tons of 20mm automatic cannon shells, 500-lb. general purpose bombs, napalm canisters, 5-inch rockets and 3.25-inch smoke rockets. In extremis, the group had stripped its El Toro Marine Corps Air Station of 352 tons of ordnance, sufficient to begin operations. Most of this was turned over to the navy in Japan for support of the carrier-based squadrons, with some cannon ammunition positioned at Itazuke for the night fighters.[17]

The communications arrangements at Itami were quickly over-taxed because the group communications section had to support General Cushman as the commanding general, 1st Marine Aircraft Wing (Forward), a role he assumed in addition to his brigade command duties. The section received 99,741 code groups in twenty-seven days before relief came in the form of a navy cryptology facility transferred from Guam, four cryptologists flown in from El Toro, and the acquisition of a Fifth Air Force teletype installation.[18]

Almost unnoticed in the shuffling of air support, the photo plane section of two F4U-5P aircraft saw little use. Flying missions out of Itazuke, it recorded thirty-five training flights but only eight initial operational flights over Korea, seven of these in the brigade's first operation near Sachon. Then, on 25 August, the section was pressed into photographic coverage of Inchon, flying thirteen sorties. It remains possible that a lack of photographic materials handicapped its operations, but in any case it provided only limited support to the brigade.

ESCORT CARRIER OPERATIONS

Rear Admiral Richard W. Ruble had offloaded antisubmarine aircraft from the *Sicily* at Guam, before sailing to Japan to join *Badoeng Strait* at Kobe for the embarkation of the two marine corps fighter squadrons. His Carrier Division 15 thus finally united for operations off the southwest coast of Korea on 6 August. Pilots of VMF-214 required no new carrier qualifications when they landed on board the *Sicily* on the third, so it began strike operations right away, the first an eight-plane attack on Chinju launched at 1638 against KPA troops. Other attacks continued against enemy troops and vehicles near Chinjui and on the Naktong front. The *Sicily* then entered the Yellow Sea, launching additional strikes launched against the Inchon-Seoul zone on 5 August, and against Kunsan and Mokpo on the sixth.[19]

Among the many pilots drawing first blood for the brigade against the enemy, Major Kenneth Reusser of VMF-214 logged in a particularly full day on 5 August. He led his flight against an industrial area near Inchon, destroying several vehicles in spite of heavy defensive fire. Suspicious of the concentration of antiaircraft fire, he left his flight orbiting at three thousand feet while he made a window level pass through the area, noting numbers of military vehicles inside the buildings. Despite taking hits on both his wings, he returned to the *Sicily* to rearm and refuel the flight. Returning to the target area, he destroyed the buildings and numerous tanks and trucks with napalm and cannon fire, then switched to Inchon harbor where the flight destroyed a large fuel storage tank. Finally, Reusser dived on an oil tanker and raked it with 20mm fire until an explosion destroyed the ship and blew his aircraft out of control. He was able to recover control and return his now crippled fighter to the ship. The Navy Cross he received for that action was the first of several dozen such awards for airmen and ground troops alike that month.[20]

Such strike operations came to a halt, however, upon receipt of MacArthur's orders to dedicate all carrier air support from 8 to 17 August to close support and interdiction in support of Eighth Army. At first, Seventh Fleet commander Vice Admiral Arthur D. Struble tried to dedicate only the escort carriers to the cumbersome tasks of coordinating with the Fifth Air Force/Eighth Army joint operations center, in order to dedicate the big carriers to hitting Seoul bridges and other strategic targets deemed to have greater value. But both he and Admiral Joy had to give way to the requirements of MacArthur's headquarters and respond to ground combat priorities. At any rate, the new priority lasted only five days and the big carriers returned to strike northern targets.[21]

Beginning 8 August, VMF-214 and VMF-323 flew priority missions in support of the combat actions of 1st Provisional Marine Brigade ground troops, that is, the 5th Marines and its attachments. With *Sicily* off-line on 10–11 August for replenishment in Sasebo, the escort carrier-based squadrons began the routine of alternating their on-station support posture for the 1st Provisional Marine Brigade and the rest of Eighth Army. These small carriers required frequent replenishment of ordnance, airplane spares, and other supplies in port. Once the carrier arrived on station, its embarked squadron would typically launch four flights of five to eight aircraft, one flight every two hours, in support of ground troops. The munitions most frequently expended were the 5-inch unguided rockets, and 500- or 1000-lb. general purpose bombs and napalm canisters. VMF-214 recorded its greatest effort on 29 August, with forty-seven sorties flown in eight strikes (every ninety minutes), expending twenty-six napalm canisters, twenty-nine 500-lb. bombs, and 208 rockets. All strikes that day supported army troops in the Pusan Perimeter, and were directed by air force airborne and army ground controllers.[22]

The sole exception to this method of support occurred during the 28 August–5 September and 1–5 September upkeep periods of *Badoeng Strait* and *Sicily*, when the squadrons had to operate from Ashiya Air Base in order to support the emergency re-employment of the brigade in its second Naktong engagement.[23]

Curiously, only the war diary of VMF-323 noted a daily combat air patrol (CAP) requirement of up to eight aircraft per day. This would have been a typical navy requirement for embarked air groups. Although air superiority had been long established, there were occasional alerts and reports of North Korean attacks on ships at sea. Several ships had not even been able to respond with on-board weapons, and no carrier skipper wanted to be so caught.[24]

In summary, while it is evident that the marine aircraft embarked on board the escort carriers remained available for support of the brigade's operations, it remains clear that the vast majority of the operations of the two fighter squadrons supported units other than the 1st Provisional Marine Brigade. Although it became politically expedient later for the marine corps to cry foul as the air force seemingly "robbed" its aircraft for the support of non-USMC ground units, the marine brigade's two Corsair squadrons flew daily, anywhere, for any mission, carrying the fight to the enemy with evident relish. VMF-323 logged in 832 flights, including 509 combat and 150 CAP missions during 5 August–5 September. VMF-214 produced 844 flights (721 combat) in August alone. Afterwards, on 6 and 8 September, the carriers with the two fighter squadrons returned to the Yellow Sea and the marine Corsairs resumed their portion of the navy strike program in support of the theater.[25]

No such division of labor came for the observation squadron (VMO-6) and the air support section of the air control squadron. The four HO3S helicopters and four OY-2 aircraft flew to Pusan (K-1 airfield) on 2 August, and upon arrival the next day of the ground echelon at Chinhae in a Japanese-crewed LST, they went into continuous operations from this Korean naval base. The air controllers established radio communications with the escort carriers sailing to the Yellow Sea on 5 August, and all was ready.

Two helos remained at all times with the brigade command post to facilitate the movements and reconnaissance needs of General Craig and his officers, while the light planes provided target spotting for aircraft and artillery as well as essential liaison tasks. Both aircraft and helicopters were pressed into action throughout the campaign for aerial resupply of units too isolated for overland methods. As ground casualties mounted, two of the helos received modifications to carry stretcher patients and continued to render the lifesaving gift of aerial medical evacuation ("medevac") that became a matter of course in Western armies a decade later.[26]

With these operational details in mind, one takes note of the incipient interservice rivalry of this period and in particular of the Korean War over control of aircraft. It remains beyond the scope of this work to explore the unending rivalries extent then and now, but the services clearly entered the Korean War with heightened sensitivities over the interservice frictions accompanying the defense reorganizations of the previous five years and, for that matter, the World War II as well. Despite the reassuring discussions by General Stratemeyer with both Generals Craig and Shepherd, who had pressed to keep marine corps aviation integral to the brigade, conflicts later surfaced over marine corps aviation public relations, despite the evident dedication of the aviators themselves to hitting the enemy under any circumstance, no holds barred.

EARLY TESTING

The Eighth Army counterattack plan approved by General Walker for a blow against the North Korean 6th Infantry Division on the southern front brought the ground troops of the 1st Provisional Marine Brigade into their first combat action. The operations plan Walker approved on 4 August called for the 25th Division to conduct the attack, in the immediate aftermath of its stiff fight with the North Korean 4th and 6th Divisions that had finally stopped the latest Korean thrust toward Pusan that very day. Although the plan called for the use of fresh reinforcements in the form of the army's 5th Regimental Combat Team and the 1st Provisional Marine Brigade, the division and its staff could hardly be considered in good shape. Hurriedly moved into the southern sector of the perimeter, it relieved a string of battered battalions of the 24th Division on 1 August but had its hands full opposing the last thrusts of the North Korean 6th Division through 4 August. By then, the front had stabilized on a north-south line extending through Chungam, Haman, and Chingdong. Occupied by the nearly exhausted troops of the division's 35th, 24th, and 27th Infantry Regiments, this position the last line of hills covering Masan. It also represented the shortest distance to the sea for any of Kim Il Sung's troops, following the Naktong River's eastward turn toward its estuary just west of Pusan.

More recently arrived than the sorely tested U.S. 24th Infantry Division, the 25th had participated in the withdrawals south from Sangju to Taegu during the 20 July–30 July period, and had not been able to halt the enemy advance on the central front. Building upon the scattered resistance of the 24th Division as the new Pusan southern front took form, the 25th did manage some tough fighting that halted the advance of and fairly decimated the North Korean 6th Division.

With RCT 5 already assembled west of Masan, the 1st Provisional Marine Brigade completed the counterattack force, now designated Task Force Kean under the 25th Division commander, Major General William B. Kean. Kean's plan consisted of a preliminary attack on 7 August by his northernmost regiment, the 35th Infantry, directed westward astride the Chinju road, but halting at the road junction of Muchon. On the southern flank, the 5th Marines would relieve the battered but successful 27th Infantry (unfortunately passing out of the operation into Eighth Army reserve), then attack alongside the RCT 5, which veered northwest to link with the 35th Infantry, leaving the 5th Marines to march via Kosong to Sachon, thus clearing the coastal route of enemy forces while army regiments took Chinju, the planned objective.

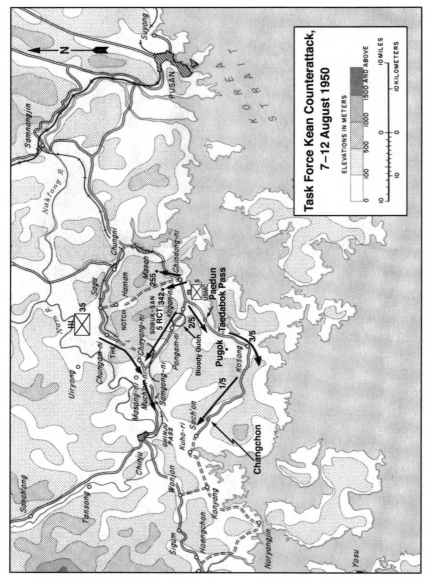

Army Map Service, printed in Appleman, *South to the Naktong, North to the Yalu: June–November, 1950.* Modified by W. Stephen Hill. The notation "1/5" (and so forth) in this and subsequesnt maps refers to 1st Battalion, 5th Marines (and so forth).

In the task force center, the 24th Infantry was to clear the area left behind *and between* the 35th Infantry and RCT 5 advance. This modest plan would assist the Eighth Army by weakening the enemy forces on the southern front and drawing his reinforcements from the Taegu area, where the major enemy threat now loomed.

This Eighth Army plan remained a limited-objective attack, followed by a return to defensive lines west of Masan, in its final form ordered on 6 August. The Eighth Army plans section continued to work on an additional plan to exploit the possible success of Task Force Kean, but the plan was obviated by unfavorable circumstances and the unavailability of troops. The limited nature of the counter-offensive apparently was never communicated to the marine brigade's leaders.[27]

Further complicating matters for the incoming marines was the failure of the 25th Division to mop up its last battlefield. As a result, the surviving elements of the North Korean 6th Infantry Division remained ensconced near and between the American positions. The records show the increasing confusion of the marine corps units as they began fighting organized enemy units in midst of occupying their attack positions, even before they were slated to attack under their planned offensive with Task Force Kean.

The reasons for this failure lay in organizational details of the 25th Division, but also in the combat skills of the U.S. Army at the time. The 25th Infantry Division was, on paper at any rate, the strongest of MacArthur's divisions in the Japan occupation force. Yet it had contributed men to fill out the 24th Infantry Division as the latter set out first on its particular odyssey in Korea during July. The reason for MacArthur's favoring the 24th Infantry Division may be attributable to one of the infantry regiments in the 25th Division, the 24th Infantry. It is seldom pointed out that the 24th Infantry was the last major African-American ("Negro" in the vernacular of the time) formation of the army. This relic of the old army, rendered obsolete by President Truman's 1948 executive order to integrate the forces, reflected the curious army concept that troops were troops, but great leaders made them into great units. Sadly, the mostly white officers of the 24th had little such effect, and the 24th had proven most unsteady in earlier action, occasionally holding up, but at other times having whole battalions recoil in panic three or four miles to the rear without orders. On 9 September, General Kean tried to remove it from further service in the Eighth Army, but it was not dissolved until a year later, with its soldiers properly integrated into other regiments as replacements.[28]

The other, more general aspect of the army that would be encountered was not the "bug-out" habit so commonly derided by members of the marine brigade. After all, the entire Eighth Army had been conducting a series of withdrawals in face of an enemy usually more numerous and always more aggressive. There was, however, another more deeply entrenched problem not yet recognized nor corrected in the U.S. Army.

During the 1941–45 Pacific War, it soon became apparent that infantry units, trained in the United States for battles of maneuver supported by artillery, tanks, and air power, lacked the basic skills and motivation to fight the Japanese infantry in close combat. The Japanese, on the other hand, lacked the industrial capacity for such tactical doctrine and instead relied upon turning and flanking maneuvers, night attacks, and close combat with the bayonet. Both of MacArthur's field army commanders during the war, Robert Eichelberger and Walter Kreuger, found that U.S. Army infantry commanders relied upon artillery to do the work of the infantry and that such doctrine had evolved into a dependency. The infantry lacked the motivation to close with and kill the enemy. Patrols, in particular, often resorted to "hiding out" and "fairy tales" instead of probing an enemy deemed too dangerous in the field.[29]

It is not difficult imagine that the soldiers of MacArthur's army showed the same tendencies given the stand-down that occupation duty in Japan represented. Considering as well the ongoing sacrifice of raw and untrained draftees and new replacements fed into the infantry units of the embattled Eighth Army, one can surmise that dealing with the hardened peasant soldiers of the KPA remained just as problematic for U.S infantrymen as had the Japanese emperor's soldiers a mere five years earlier.

Moreover, it is just such a doctrinal flaw that would explain the continuing presence after 4 August of the North Korean 6th Division in the hills of the Sobuk mining region, stretching *between* the forward positions of the 35th Infantry in the north and those of the 27th Infantry on the coastal road forming the southern anchor of Eighth Army lines. The 25th Infantry Division's defensive sector in fact bowed eastward around this inhospitable terrain feature, and the

24th Infantry remained the least likely unit to rout the enemy troops from this natural redoubt. Patrols of the 25th Infantry Division in the same vein had little chance of discovering the enemy in their midst, given the halfhearted execution of such tactical measures to date in the campaign.

The enemy thus proved most uncooperative. Sensing that their best moment to eject U.N. forces was slipping away, the North Koreans redoubled their efforts, spurring their exhausted troops to overcome the defenders before the odds shifted decisively against them.

INTO THE BREACH, THE FIRST TIME

General Walker activated Task Force Kean for the operation on 6 August, tasking it with attacking toward Chinju and relieving pressure on Masan. His orders specified 0630 on 7 August as "H-hour" for initiating the attack. As the fresh reinforcements to the task force passed through the 27th Infantry, that unit would revert to army reserve with priority of planning going to the 24th Infantry Division sector. Kean ordered General Craig to effect the relief of 27th Infantry, assuming command of the sector as soon as he had two battalions in place.[30]

The 5th Marines trucked from the Changwon encampment beginning at 1040 on 6 August, with 3rd Battalion, 5th Marines in the lead. Lieutenant Colonel Taplett relieved the army's 1st Battalion, 27th Infantry (the regiment's tactical reserve) at 1547 in its position near Chingdong. The remainder of the 5th Marines continued through the night of 6–7 August using the same trucks that took 3rd Battalion, 5th Marines forward. The 2nd Battalion, 5th Marines arrived at Chingdong about 0500, followed by Lieutenant Colonel Murray's command group and then General Craig's.

By this time, the shuttling of the trucks had turned the village into mire, especially a schoolyard used for the turnaround of the truck columns. Sporadic shell and mortar fire had continued to fall on the village since the arrival of 3rd Battalion, 5th Marines, adding to the already chaotic scene. General Craig and Lieutenant Colonel Murray directed the deployment of the two battalions into adjacent hills, and awaited the advance of RCT 5, which had to clear the fork in the road in order to allow the brigade to move toward Suchon via Kosong. Adding to this complicated assembly of units in the Task Force Kean counterattack, a battalion of RCT 5 had reinforced the lines of the

27th Infantry on 2 August, coming straight off the docks of Pusan port. While the 27th Infantry held terrain west of Chingdong in the intended direction of attack, RCT 5's 2nd Battalion held the northern flank of this indistinct jumping-off point where three disparate regiments of Task Force Kean were expected to conduct a passage of lines, relief in place, and a tactical withdrawal, all as part of the same "offensive."

This was not to be. Already, a platoon of the 3rd Battalion, 5th Marines had been ordered up by 27th Infantry to reinforce F Company, 2nd Battalion, 5th Infantry on Hill 342. This company had been defending in place since 3 August, already losing and recovering the exposed position once. With some protests, Lieutenant Colonel Taplett gave up his battalion reserve (3rd platoon, G Company, commanded by First Lieutenant John H. J. Cahill), sending it forward during the night into the array of army units jammed into the nest of hills surrounding the road junction west of Chingdong. Climbing in daylight against sporadic small-arms fire as the heat of 7 August built, the platoon managed to join the battered F Company and assisted it in holding out for another twenty-four hours under fire. The marines had taken some casualties climbing the trail, then spread out to bolster the army troops, spending the rest of the day pinned down by small-arms fire under the glaring sun. Marines and soldiers spent the next day, 8 August, fighting off KPA assaults until relieved by D Company of Lieutenant Colonel Harold Roise's 2nd Battalion, 5th Marines. First Lieutenant Bone, Cahill's company commander, remarked, "It took a hell of a long time to get Cahill out of there. When he rejoined the company, it was a very dramatic time. Jesus, he cried and I cried. He'd lost a lot of people."[31]

Hill 342 was merely an extension of the long ridgeline descending in several fingers south from Sobuk (Hill 738), and the North Korean 6th Division now sent its own attack streaming down the slopes into the American forces. Pandemonium ensued as attackers became the attacked on each side. More enemy artillery fire fell into the brigade's units in the narrow valley floor while the infantry battalions of the 5th Marines occupied and defended the high ground to the west and north.[32]

Still, the planned advance went forward into an already calamitous situation. The lead battalion of RCT 5 moved out at 0720 and blundered down the wrong road, the one allocated to the marine brigade, while Roise's 2nd Battalion moved up to relieve the embattled 2nd Battalion, 5th Infantry.

Taking charge of the sector at 1120 upon the final relief of the 27th Infantry, General Craig ordered the last battalion of the 5th Marines into action: Lieutenant Colonel Newton's 1st Battalion, 5th Marines moved in the assigned direction of the marine attack, only to halt while the 1st Battalion, 5th Infantry blocked his intended route. Completing the chaos, Taplett's 3rd Battalion, 5th Marines had to react to new North Korean moves to the east, which included a roadblock set up by the enemy on the road back to Masan.

Instead of the fluid advance called for in the plans for Task Force Kean, the 7–8 August actions produced confusion between American forces still sorting themselves out among the hills surrounding Ching-dong, and the advancing troops of the enemy 6th Division pushing down the slopes of the Subok position toward the Masan road. All three battalions of the 5th Marines required all of 8 August and part of the following day to sort out their positions and to turn back their share of the enemy attack. The 3rd Battalion, 5th Marines and elements of two battalions of the 24th Infantry attacked to restore control of Hill 255 and the road to Masan after repeated assaults and artillery bombardment.

The relief of the 2nd Battalion, 5th Infantry required a repeat attack by the 2nd Battalion, 5th Marines on 9 August to clear enemy resistance on both sides of Hill 342. In similar fashion, the 3rd Battalion, 5th Marines unsuccessfully attacked Hill 255 on 8 August, but finished the job the next day. In each case, enemy resistance required both air strikes and artillery barrages before the two-company battalions of the 5th Marines could prevail. Summing up the day's frustrations, the antitank (recoilless rifle) company reported being "strafed by our own Corsairs. No casualties."[33]

The fighting was so stiff on Hill 255 that H Company riflemen received a Navy Cross and three Army Distinguished Service Crosses for their first day's effort. Staff Sergeant James Davis led his platoon within seventy-five yards of entrenched North Koreans only to die from a defective hand grenade. Nearby, Corporal Melvin James rallied his squad on the bare ridgeline, regaining enough fire superiority to continue forward and keep the company's skirmish line intact. Later, he retrieved six wounded comrades and delivered them into the hands of the hospital corpsmen. Not so lucky was another squad leader,

Corporal Joseph J. Batluck, who also rallied his men and rescued wounded, but was killed in doing so. As acting platoon sergeant, Jack E. Macy fell back with his platoon near the end of the day, only to discover that he could not account for three of his men. Searching the ground under heavy fire, he located and gave first aid to the wounded soldiers, then carried each of them to safety. On yet a fourth trip to retrieve a fallen comrade's body, he was ordered to cover it up and leave it in place.[34]

The army units had some success as well on 9 August, and the nearly exhausted 2nd Battalion, 5th Infantry managed to clear the way out of Chingdong road junction on the planned northeast route toward the road junction of Muchon, where the 35th Infantry awaited it. With this reshuffling the 1st Battalion, 5th Infantry cleared out of the marine brigade's direction of attack, and the way remained clear for the planned advance of Task Force Kean after three full days of interference by the North Korean 6th Division.

The actions of 7–9 August demonstrate that all American units encountered difficulties in maneuvering against a tough opponent in exhausting terrain amid sapping heat. In its first series of combat engagements, the 5th Marines responded well to a baffling array of surprises that caused its infantry battalions to attack narrow objectives in three different directions. Flesh and bone gave way under such duress and some objectives given to the men proved more than could be handled. Both the 2nd Battalion and 3rd Battalions of the 5th Marines stalled in their attacks of 8 August and required repeat efforts the next day to clear away the enemy, after employing artillery and air support. Lieutenant Colonel Taplett recalled in his memoirs that he relieved a rifle platoon leader in his battalion's H Company for failing to move into the attack. Such an incident can only be assumed as one of several typical "awakening moments" of a green unit in its first fight. Combat does naturally sort out these matters, provided a unit has moments to pause and reset itself.[35]

Duplicating the army's mistaken opening moves out of Chingdong on 7 August, George Newton's 1st Battalion, 5th Marines took the wrong road as it led the brigade out of the road junction in the early morning hours of 9 August, while its sister infantry battalions still fought to clear the northern flank of the brigade position. Freed by General Kean from further responsibilities for army troops in the

Chingdong sector, Craig could concentrate on his own planned advance. In this case, no further enemy forces revealed themselves and Newton's battalion changed routes without incident, halting at 1600 on its objective after covering two miles on the road to Kosong. General Craig noted in his field notebook, "This Bn very slow and required much pushing by me against only light resistance." Returning to his command post, he ordered Lieutenant Colonel Murray to continue the advance with a night march. Yet Captain Francis Fenton of Newton's B Company recalled in great detail the difficulties of moving forward with his weary men. Perilously short of water and having been on their feet since the night of 7–8 August, many succumbed to heat exhaustion along the road.[36]

The continuation of the brigade's advance into the night of 9 August fell to the equally weary men of the 2nd Battalion, 5th Marines. Finally relieved from their positions around Hill 342 at 1600, they now mounted trucks to return to an assembly area on the main route behind 1st Battalion, 5th Marines. Passing through that battalion around 0115 on the 10th, Roise's battalion neared Paedun, meeting no resistance. This was a night march, as the general had ordered, not a night attack. Beginning at 0600, 1st Battalion, 5th Marines resumed the march, followed in trace of Roise's men. The brigade command post, the bulk of the tank company, and the artillery of 1st Battalion, 11th Marines all followed the infantry along the road.

At 0500, one of the M26 tanks accompanying the lead riflemen collapsed the concrete bridge in the act of crossing it. The second tank, also from Lieutenant William Pomeroy's 1st Platoon, then threw its track in the stream bed as the march column bypassed the fallen bridge. Although the advance seemed in jeopardy, engineers and civilian labor gangs made new crossings for light vehicles and later extracted the second tank and built a fording site for heavier vehicles. The tank jammed in the fallen single-span bridge had to be stripped, abandoned, and destroyed with explosives. Reaching Paedun at 0800 and finding it deserted, 2nd Battalion, 5th Marines reformed and resumed its march at 0930 toward Kosong.

Generals Kean and Craig both harried their commands to speed up the advance, hoping to recover the momentum and timing lost at Chingdong and the collision with the enemy's 6th Division there. In response to Craig's prodding, trucks and jeeps were assembled to move the advance guard immediately toward Kosong, followed by the operable three tanks of Pomeroy's platoon. After a two-mile advance, the jeep-mounted reconnaissance detachment hit an ambush in the Taedabok Pass before Pugok and the advance guard came under rifle, machine-gun, and light mortar fire. With the three tanks coming up to add their support, the marines resolved the firefight in favor of D Company, 2nd Battalion, 5th Marines. The advance resumed after this two-hour episode, but Lieutenant Colonel Murray had already ordered up Taplett's 3rd Battalion, 5th Marines, newly arrived at Paedun in trucks after turning over its Hill 255 positions that day.

The situation became confused as Taplett de-trucked his men at Taedabok Pass just as the rest of the 2nd Battalion, 5th Marines caught up on foot to join its motorized advance guard. Murray ordered Taplett to pass through 2nd Battalion's forward units to continue the attack toward Kosong, now visible a mere five miles to the south from the high ground that D Company had seized. G Company, under First Lieutenant Bone, prepared to attack the hill covering a bend in the road, but the 2nd Battalion still had no sense of where the enemy positions now lay. Anxious to resolve the situation, Roise's operations officer, Major Morgan B. McNeely, took a radio jeep and a couple of riflemen from D Company to round the bend and reconnoiter the situation. A flurry of small-arms and machine-gun fire erupted as the jeep curved out of sight. G Company attacked into the fray and one of Bone's platoons flanked the enemy to the north. McNeely and two men were killed in the fusillade and two more lay wounded as both G and H Companies set in at 2025 on each side of the road. By nightfall the 3rd Battalion held its positions with the wrecked jeep marking no man's land.[37]

As the battalion prepared to resume its advance at 0800 the next day, 11 August, a melee developed when some North Korean soldiers rushed the G Company's positions. The skirmish ended much to the marines' advantage, and the battalion moved down the road toward Kosong encountering no further resistance. The leading platoon of G Company moved fast as the road dropped out of the pass. Skirmishers literally ran through the foliage flanking each side of the road while the main body moved a little more slowly. These maneuvers enabled the marines to envelop several North Korean machine-gun positions set up to delay their advance.

The reason for the enemy's failed efforts soon became clear. As Taplett's men debouched into the valley floor and approached Kosong, the artillery forward observers accompanying them called fire on the crossroads west of the town in order to register the howitzers of the 1st Battalion, 11th Marines. The 105mm rounds impacted so close to camouflaged North Korean vehicles that the enemy believed they had been spotted and immediately began to withdraw in a jumbled column estimated as eight miles long.

These vehicles constituted the main body of the North Korean 83rd Motorized Regiment, 105th Armored Division, which had been ordered up in support of the enemy's 6th Infantry Division. But its nearly two hundred "thin-skinned" trucks, cars, and motorcycles had not participated in the 6th Division's attack out of the Sobuk hills, probably because the terrain was unsuited for motorized operations. In any event, the enemy vehicles now broke cover in full view of the advancing 3rd Battalion marines and under the guns of the 1st Battalion, 11th Marines and, most disastrously for the North Koreans, under the wings of the F4U Corsairs of VMF-323, flying routine close air support for the morning's advance. In what became known as the "Kosong Turkey Shoot," the pilots mauled the enemy column, destroying about forty vehicles. Two F4Us went down under enemy fire, so close and savage was the fray, one pilot being killed. But a relief flight of Corsairs and another of air force F-51 Mustang fighters continued the pounding. One account reported thirty-one trucks, twenty-four jeeps, and forty-five motorcycles destroyed in the strike area, with the remainder of an estimated two battalions retreating into the nearby hills or toward Sachon.

Taplett's men continued their march through Kosong, H Company on the road to Suchon and G Company against enemy positions discovered on Hill 88 to the southwest of the town. Once again the marine artillery and air support brought down a deadly rain of steel and fire, and G Company found only traces of a fleeing opponent when they reached the crest at 1330. General Craig, present again to observe the leading troops, ordered Taplett to resume the advance, and H Company and a section of M26s from the 2nd platoon of the tank company headed west on the road. Almost immediately they encountered two 45mm antitank guns, but the two tanks eliminated them with six rounds of 90mm fire. The enemy could offer little in the way of rear guard resistance, and the 3rd Battalion continued a full four miles from Kosong before halting at 1700 to prepare night positions.

With the capture of Kosong, the marine brigade had at last showed its full offensive potential. The infantry battalions would advance in column, passing the freshest into the lead, with artillery, tank, and air support continually available, and with the length of the column providing good flanking protection from enemy stragglers in the neighboring hills. One infantry battalion always brought up the rear. The Kosong position also brought the brigade to its closest point to the sea. Experienced amphibious troops always take advantage of proximity to the sea, and the navy brought in LSTs to Tangdong to land service units and build supply dumps. Such support gave the brigade even more confidence in its advance. The enemy had been dislodged from the passes and continued now in full retreat.

On 12 August, the brigade command post moved to Kosong at 0800 while the 1st Battalion, 5th Marines stepped off at 0630 in the advance, using a motorized advance guard as before, passing through the positions of the 3rd Battalion, 5th Marines at 0700. Nothing happened for the first four and a half hours and the 1st Battalion covered eleven miles, entering Changchon four miles short of Sachon. Here, it turned out, elements from the survivors of the KPA 83rd Motorized Regiment and troops of 15th Regiment, 6th Infantry Division had entrenched in the hills overlooking the valley floor.

Things would have been worse had the enemy waited for the entire battalion column to pass into the ambuscade, but instead his machine guns opened up on the leading elements. While the two rifle companies deployed off the road to each flank, the 3rd Platoon of the tank company, commanded by veteran First Lieutenant G. G. Sweet, moved forward into the fire zone, keeping to the road to avoid bogs. In a four-and-a-half-hour engagement, the tanks fired to the front (toward the village) and to each side, while A Company maneuvered across Hills 301 and 250 to clear the right flank and riflemen of B Company took the long ridgeline of Hill 202 on the left. As mortar crews and artillerymen heaved and strained to bring their weapons to bear, the Corsairs roared into action. The aircraft pummeled Hill 250 with bombs and 20mm cannon fire, and then the artillery and mortars rained steel on the other two hills. More flights of F4Us returned from the carriers to strike the hills. By nightfall, A Company held the high ground to the east and B Company was still setting in on its ridgeline to the east. Leading his squad on the right flank of A Company, Corporal Donald D. Sowl and his men uncovered an enemy position that threatened the entire company flank. Despite a bullet impact that broke his upper arm, Sowl reoriented his squad and assaulted the position, driving its occupants off as his company took its objective.

Although the enemy had occupied a menacing position, it became clear that no more than a company of enemy troops had been used to delay the marine advance. Although friendly losses totaled three killed, two missing, and thirteen wounded, a significant enemy blocking position had fallen to Lieutenant Colonel Newton and his men.

The way to Sachon now seemed clear, but already problems beyond the control of the marine brigade began to affect its operations—a circumstance that would become all too characteristic of its campaign in Korea.

Although the initial movements of the army's RCT 5 out of Chingdong began in a promising manner, the regiment did not achieve the success enjoyed by the marine brigade on the southern route of Kasong-Sachon. Instead, it cut into the heart of the North Korean 6th Division's dispositions in the Subok zone, and the enemy quickly demonstrated that he was still full of fight. While easily holding off the advance of the 24th Infantry from the east, the North Koreans staged a major battle for the pass at Pogam. Here, the U.S. Army infantry occupied the hills overlooking the pass to its north and southeast flanks on 10 August, while its two artillery battalions emplaced in open ground on the road leading into the pass, near the regimental command post. One infantry battalion continued through the pass and halted to prepare for the next day's advance. But that night (10–11 August), North Korean troops attacked the north flank, where the enemy retained a foothold not occupied by RCT 5 infantry. Just as at Chingdong, that hill position was the terminus of a long finger reaching north to the main 6th Division positions on the Subok. During the night several artillery batteries came under attack as well.

On 11 August, the army infantry cleared the remaining positions on its north flank and continued to move through the pass, under pressure from General Kean to press onward with the planned offensive and link up with the 35th Infantry in the process. The 25th Infantry Division intelligence staff still believed that no significant enemy forces lay in the vicinity of Pongam, despite the reports from RCT 5.

Thus the stage was set for the disastrous fight in what became known as Bloody Gulch. With the second of the three army infantry battalions continuing through the pass on the night of 11–12 August, only one battalion held the high ground on both flanks of Pongam, and no infantry covered the artillery that waited to move out the next day. The North Koreans knew the location of the now unprotected artillery and launched coordinated attacks, supported by tanks, to pin the infantry in the hills while they savaged the batteries of the 555th and 90th Field Artillery Battalions. The commander of RCT 5, who would be soon relieved of his duties, lost control of the situation, and the KPA 13th Regiment continued its attack in daylight against the artillery in the so-called Bloody Gulch river bed. Although some of its 105mm guns continued to fire as late as 0900, the 555th was overrun (less one of its batteries already forward with the infantry that had crossed the pass). The 155mm battery and headquarters of the 90th suffered the same fate, withdrawing without their guns after 0900. The first flight of Corsairs on station made attacks against observed enemy positions, as did some F-51s, but without ground controllers or tactical commanders on the scene, the air strikes were largely ineffective.[38]

While the artillery was being overrun in Bloody Gulch, however, the two infantry battalions of RCT 5 made it with little problem to the 35th Infantry lines at Muchon. On 13 August they continued as planned to the Chinju Pass, from which they viewed the Task Force Kean's objective a few miles in the distance. But it was all for naught, as the operational situation remained untenable. The North Korean 6th Infantry Division held stubbornly to its positions in and around Subok.[39]

General Craig first learned of the setbacks at 1130 on the 12th, while reporting to the division commander, and just as the 1st Battalion, 5th Marines ran into the enemy roadblock at Changchon. General Kean ordered Craig to send a reinforced infantry battalion immediately to the rear to assist the 24th Infantry in restoring the situation. In an episode that would soon become typical of marine operations in Korean, the brigade's helicopters provided extraordinary advantage to the force, enabling Craig to fly immediately to confer with Lieutenant Colonels Murray and Taplett at the 5th Marines command post on the Sachon road, twice stopping en route on the road to order trucks to drop their cargos and proceed to pick up the 3rd Battalion, 5th Marines. He then sent his own operations officer and Taplett in the helo to the Bloody Gulch to assess the situation. Craig took another helicopter forward to visit 1st Battalion and satisfy himself that its situation remained under control. The 5th Marines went into night positions except for the 3rd Battalion, which would operate under tactical direction of the 25th Infantry Division. Summoned to meet with Kean at Masan, Craig flew to the latter's command post at 1730, passing over the lead elements of the 3rd Battalion as they moved into the position of the overrun 90th Field Artillery.[40]

A day that had begun so auspiciously for the 1st Provisional Marine Brigade had become progressively more problematic by the time Craig arrived for his meeting with Kean. With the situation in Bloody Gulch still not entirely resolved (thanks to the disaster that befell RCT 5), he was now informed by Kean that the marine brigade was to detach immediately from the 25th Division. The counterattack mission of Task Force Kean had been cancelled by General Walker because the North Koreans had assaulted the Naktong River defenses of the 24th Infantry Division, crossing the river and establishing a bridgehead on the opposite shore that now threatened the rear of Eighth Army itself.

The withdrawal began on 13 August, after Craig issued his orders from his own command post at Kosong. He ordered the 1st Battalion, 5th Marines back through the lines of Roise's 2nd Battalion, now the designated rear guard for the brigade. In the predawn hours on 14 August, a number of North Korean troops crept up on the position of B Company on Hill 202. At 0415 they launched an unusually effective close assault against the 3rd Platoon, on the company's left flank, overrunning that unit and its attached machine-gun squad. A supporting attack against the other two platoons, accompanied by heavy machine-gun, small-arms, and mortar fire, was beaten back with difficulty. Four marines were wounded in the fray, among them Private First Class Herbert E. Fear, hit in the shoulder. Refusing medical aid, Fear covered the evacuation of his wounded buddies, killing three North Korean soldiers who rushed their position and turning away several others by his determined resistance. Hit yet again by mortar fragments, he continued to hold his position until his squad had fallen back, rejoining them only to fall unconscious from loss of blood. Shortly thereafter, Sergeant Malcom L. Budd, the B Company telephonic wire chief, saw a man in the company rear guard fall wounded. Crossing fifty yards of open ground under enemy fire, he hefted the man into a fireman's carry, only to be cut down and killed by a burst of machine-gun fire.

The marine corps official history failed to explain this enemy success, but no less an authority than Francis I. Fenton, Jr., the company executive officer at the time, stated over a year later that the company was exhausted by the day's efforts, and unwisely elected to maintain a 50 percent alert through the night that was simply beyond human endurance. Ideally, in each two-man fighting position one man would stay awake while the other slept. But the fatigue was general and hard to resist, and in too many instances both men occupying a fighting position were sound asleep when the North Koreans attacked. In consequence the 1st Battalion suffered fifty-six casualties: fifteen killed, thirty-three wounded, and eight missing. The bodies of the two missing machine-gun teams would not be recovered until the Pusan breakout after 15 September. It was an ignominious end to the Sachon counteroffensive, and a sharp reminder (as if the marines needed one) of the enemy's tenacity.[41]

While the brigade collected itself and marched back toward Masan, the 3rd Battalion, 5th Marines operated briefly on its own as the first relief unit to reach Bloody Gulch and then began the recovery of the RCT 5 artillery park there. Lieutenant Colonel Taplett's battalion reached its ordered Chingdong assembly area at 1645. Moving tactically to the north with his companies in column, Taplett secured the area around the surviving 159th Field Artillery Battalion, and soon his own artillery of C Battery, 1st Battalion, 11th Marines, joined his marines a mile short of Bloody Gulch and held that position overnight 13–14 August without incident. At daybreak, the marines moved through the devastated area where the two army artillery units had been overrun. They found no enemy in this site and were relieved at 1430 on 14 August by the 2nd Battalion, 5th Infantry. This was the same unit that Taplett's battalion had contacted and reinforced on arrival as the 1st Provisional Marine Brigade's lead formation on 6 August, whence the whole operation had begun for the brigade with the dispatch of Lieutenant Cahill's platoon to assist in holding Hill 342.

Assessing the Brigade's First Fight

Air support from the two Corsair squadrons gave crucial boosts to the infantrymen of the 5th Marines in several instances already noted. Although the two escort carriers of Carrier Group 15 launched almost all missions in support of the brigade while the latter was engaged in combat in its drive from Chingdong to Sachon, the aircraft did not strike targets exclusively in the brigade's area of operations. Furthermore, the sorties of VMF-214 and 323 were not the only air support flown for the brigade, as the air force recorded 100 of its 364 sorties on August 8 as being flown in support of the 25th Division.[42]

A snapshot of squadron operations reveals that marine corps flights were launched in sequence so as to provide continuous air support over the brigade's position during daylight hours. On 8 August, VMF-214 launched flights of four aircraft each at 0630, 1130, and 1600, and VMF-323 launched a tactical air controller (TAC) two-plane flight at 0630 and three strike flights after 0800, all hitting targets northwest of Chingdong. The air controller flights carried smoke rockets for marking targets for the strike aircraft, and VMF-323 probably performed this duty as well as providing the combat air patrol missions over the carriers (eight that day) because its carrier served as the task force flagship during the campaign.

The following day saw a virtual repeat of the previous day's air operations, with a total of twenty-five sorties from *Sicily* by VMF-214 and nineteen from *Badoeng Strait* by VMF-323, as well as six sorties for combat air patrol duties. *Sicily* then returned to Sasebo for replenishment and the next two days saw a maximum effort by VMF-323 as the 5th Marines pushed through roadblocks and through Kosong as well. Here the squadron showed its mettle, for it had lagged behind VMF-214 in carrier competencies since MAG-33 had formed for this campaign.

Starting at 0630 on 10 August, VMF-323 launched eight flights of five to six aircraft each, including an airborne controller aircraft, which operated until the last recovery at 2000. In the first flight, Captain Vivian M. Moses, the flight leader, had to ditch his airplane in the sea after taking ground fire. He was rescued by a helicopter from VMO-6. The next day, nine flights of three to five aircraft each launched from *Badoeng Strait* between 0630–1700 (with the combat air patrol over the carriers typically covering 0628–2007). The five-plane flight at 1230 and the four-plane launch at 1400 executed the "Kosong Turkey Shoot" against the fleeing vehicles of the North Korean 83rd Motorized Regiment; the remaining three flights of the day hit only a few vehicles that could be spotted. One of the most impressive actions had to be that of Captain Moses. He returned to the carrier via helicopter at 1300 and then led the flight launching at 1400, only to be killed when enemy ground fire downed two of the F4Us. He was the first pilot lost in action by MAG-33, and the Distinguished Flying Cross awarded to him posthumously on 27 December 1950 was one of the first of the Korean War.[43]

Both carriers operated on 12 July, putting forty-five sorties over the brigade, and then *Badoeng Strait* entered Sasebo that evening for her replenishment. VMF-214 then flew an impressive thirty-four strike sorties on 13 August as the brigade withdrew its ground forces from the front.[44]

Later in the Korean War, much emphasis would be made of marine corps air support and the "proper" use of it as part of an "integrated air-ground team." At this juncture, it remains noteworthy that the marine corps aircraft sorties flown for the brigade covered less than a week of operations, during which they also ranged freely across the battlefields, supporting adjacent army units and flying interdiction strikes at more distant targets, especially when no targets appeared during the missions covering the brigade (unused bombs and rockets otherwise were jettisoned before recovering the aircraft on board the carriers). Thus the air-ground team had yet to be defined in terms of its actions. The two day fighter squadrons flew approximately one thousand sorties each during August, supporting many U.N. forces. The night fighter squadron operated for the Fifth Air Force and the photo reconnaissance detachment took no part in the initial battles. In no sense were marine corps F4U sorties launched solely for support of marine corps ground operations.

Conventional support by the artillery battalion, 1st Battalion, 11th Marines, continued throughout the Suchon operation, handicapped only by narrow defiles and periodic lack of off-road space to deploy and set up the twelve 105mm howitzers of the three firing batteries. During the Chingdong phase of the operation, they fired eighty-nine missions, expending 1,829 rounds of ammunition. During the 10–13 August drive on Suchon, the marine corps cannoneers fired another seventy-five missions in which they expended 1,597 rounds. Operating near the end of the brigade column, the artillery had to leapfrog its firing batteries to stay within supporting distance, and then detach C Battery to accompany 3rd Battalion, 5th Marines in its move to Bloody Gulch.

As General Craig's brigade filed past his old command post at Chingdong, he mused over the apparent waste of precious men in a movement cancelled within sight of the brigade's initial objective,

Suchon, and with the army equally in sight of the task force objective at Chunju.

The brigade's first dose of combat produced a considerable season-ing, or "shaking out," after its offload and assembly. The enemy had been met and defeated, marines were sure to see, yet the operation had been cancelled and the ground gained had been given up. Was the army just not up to the effort? Craig's field journal noted, "During period 7–13 Aug we had 58 KIA, 7 DOW, and 229 WIA. Total 66 KIA."[45]

We now know that the Eighth Army staff had only envisioned a limited-objective attack and harbored little hope for retaining any of the ground gained by Task Force Kean. The marine brigade had been forced to assist RCT 5 and the 27th Infantry in an unplanned fight for the jumping off points ("attack positions," in doctrinal parlance) at Chingdong, yet it was not at all clear at the time that the North Korean 6th Division was attacking in its own right or that the efforts of Task Force Kean therefore generated a spoiling attack that removed the 6th Division as an offensive threat to Masan, at least for the moment. The more ambitious aim of executing a counterattack and threatening the southern flank of the Korean People's Army therefore never could be achieved, and it remains likely that North Koreans sent not a single soldier south nor weakened in any way their major offensive aimed at Taegu. Craig might have been even more dismayed had he known that his brigade's efforts had simply served to buy more time for the Eighth Army to build its defenses.

In summary, the 1st Provisional Marine Brigade assisted the army in tidying up the battlefield at Chingdong, then marched on the Suchon road in a column of battalions, and overcame a succession of outposts covering the assembly area of the North Korean 85th Motorized Regiment in the Kosong-Suchon area. Left unmolested, that motorized regiment would have been held in reserve until North Korean 6th Division took Masan, after which the terrain leading to Pusan would have proved ideal for a quick thrust to cut the U.N. supply lines, dooming the Pusan Perimeter as a tenable position.

For now, the marines had taken the 85th Motorized Regiment out of the enemy's order of battle. But another mission and even deadlier struggle loomed as marines loaded trucks and trains destined for another part of the front, where yet another series of enemy-held hills awaited them.

3

Naktong Battles

Fresh from its baptism by fire, The 1st Provisional Marine Brigade proceeded to make its key contributions to the defense of the Pusan Perimeter with two sharp combat actions in virtually the same piece of terrain, shoring up the collapsing Naktong Bulge defenses and throwing the enemy back. These actions forged the reputation of the formation as a "fire brigade" and gave birth to marine corps lore that credited the brigade with saving the U.S. Army from a disastrous defeat.

Although the geography of the Korean Peninsula is generally forbidding from a military standpoint, the terrain in the Pusan Perimeter practically defies description in terms of the difficulties it poses to conducting both defensive and offensive operations. This last defensible position into which the Eighth Army had withdrawn at the end of July used the Naktong River to anchor much of its one hundred air-mile western face. After the lower Naktong turned eastward toward the Sea of Japan (thus leaving a "bulge" protruding to the west), the mountains around Sobuk anchored the last thirty-five miles of U.N. lines extending southward to the Yellow Sea. Farther north on the Naktong lay Taegu, the major city (pop. 355,000) anchoring the center of the Eighth Army positions. It stood astride the lines of communication into the region from the north and west of the Republic of Korea. Its importance increased when it became the temporary seat of the

South Korean government and field army headquarters, as well as General Walker's Eighth Army headquarters.

Most importantly, Taegu contained the northwest corner of the coastal and inland circular road and rail network over which the vital logistics and reinforcements landed at the port of Pusan flowed to the defending U.N. forces. North of Taegu, the South Korean Army defended the left bank of the Naktong River from Waegwan to Naktong. From there the defenses veered west into the formidable and relatively isolated coastal mountains extending some fifty air miles to Yongdok on the Sea of Japan. South Korea's remaining five reconstituted divisions thus protected the northern approaches to the Pusan Perimeter as well as covering the small but useful port of Pohang on the northeastern quadrant of the U.N. position.

Inasmuch as North Korean forces easily crossed the Naktong River in late summer, it possessed negligible value as a defensive barrier for the Eighth Army and South Korean forces. However, the river at least provided an interruption to the mountainous terrain that had proved difficult to defend and at the same time facilitated North Korean infiltration tactics. Once the immediate North Korean threat to Masan and Pusan in the south had been halted by the efforts of the 25th Infantry Division and Task Force Kean, the defense of Taegu became the paramount concern of U.N. commanders.

The North Koreans saw the battlefield in the same light and, after their quick thrusts at Masan and Pusan had been halted in August, they directed their main effort against Taegu. Beginning on 5 August and for the two weeks following, two North Korean infantry divisions supported by tanks of the 105th Armored Division pounded the South Korean 1st Division on its Naktong lines, driving it back down the natural valley approach toward Taegu. By 15 August, General Walker was forced to send help in the form of one U.S. and one South Korean infantry regiment. At the same time, the South Korean 6th Division, positioned just west of the South Korean 1st Division, received similar pressure from two additional North Korean divisions, and was forced back into the mountains where it stood off further attacks and contained the right flank of the North Korean breakthrough.

From 18–25 August, North Korean tanks and infantry attacked the U.S. 27th Infantry Regiment, which had reinforced the South Koreans and blocked the Naktong valley corridor and adjacent roadway from

Sangju to Taegu—the enemy's main axis of advance. So many attacks by North Korean infantry and tanks took place here that the U.S. soldiers nicknamed it the "Bowling Alley" because of the way the tank guns of both sides reverberated from the steep hills flanking the roadway. The last attack of this initial North Korean effort took place on 24 August.

This attack took the form of the usual night foray into the 27th Infantry positions. Two enemy infantry companies, supported by an unknown number of tanks, advanced after midnight along the poplar-fringed country road. The American infantrymen easily beat them back and artillery fire added two more tank hulks to the total of thirteen T-34 tanks, five self-propelled guns, and twenty-three other vehicles that by then dotted the valley floor. The South Korean 1st Division, which had held the flanking hills of the Bowling Alley, then relieved the 27th Infantry and held the lines for the time being, while the latter returned to the 25th Infantry Division at Masan.

Taegu remained secure, but North Korean supporting attacks on other parts of the Pusan Perimeter threatened to place the U.N. forces in equally dire straits.

To the east of the Taegu offensive, the North Koreans launched two divisions and an independent regiment in the first days of August southward on the roads to Pohang from Andong and Yongdok. Several of their regiments simply disappeared into the mountains and re-emerged south of the defenders at the very gates of the small port. The South Korean 3rd Division had defended well for two weeks, but found itself pinned against the sea, requiring eventual evacuation by the U.S. Navy. General Walker hurriedly ordered reinforcements and moved to defend Pohang, including the South Korean Capital Division and elements of the U.S. 2nd Infantry Division. Although Pohang was saved by these timely deployments, the decision was made to evacuate U.S. Air Force fighter aircraft based at Yonil to bases in Japan—a precautionary measure that correctly anticipated the desperate battles yet to come.

Just as the enemy's eastern offensive supported the main attacks on Taegu, so did the attacks across the lower reaches of the Naktong south of the city. The 1st Cavalry Division fought to hold off the attacks of two North Korean divisions and also to hold its right flank firm while the South Korean 1st Division struggled against the main attacks. In general, the defenses in the 1st Cavalry Division's sector succeeded, and it alone defeated their enemy at the Naktong crossings that proved too difficult for other units to defend.[1]

The other supporting attack of early August took place in the Naktong Bulge itself, and was directed at the army's 24th Infantry Division. Here enemy successes drew the commitment of the marine brigade from General Walker's slim Eighth Army reserve.

Task Force Kean's counterattack operation had expired on August 11, before the marine brigade had approached Suchon and while the two artillery battalions with RCT 5 experienced catastrophe at Bloody Gulch. By that time, the situation elsewhere in the perimeter had begun to rapidly deteriorate despite strenuous efforts to build the defensive power of U.N. forces. General Walker ordered General Kean that day to prepare to release at any moment both RCT 5 and the marine brigade back to Eighth Army control. At the same time, Walker ordered the 9th Infantry Regiment and a battalion of the 27th Infantry (with the rest of the regiment soon to follow) to reinforce the 24th Infantry Division as it faced North Korean troops forcing the Naktong River to its front.[2]

While the marine brigade fought under the 24th Infantry Division in the Naktong Bulge, multiple crises flared in other sectors. On 18 August, the South Korean government panicked and fled Taegu, even though the city remained under Eighth Army control and with ROK police deployed to stop the fleeing civilian population from jamming the roads. The efforts of the U.S. 23rd and 27th Infantry Regiments saved the Taegu sector, and were typical of many such uses of reinforced regiments as "fire brigades" all along Eighth Army's positions.[3]

The 24th Infantry Division's battle for the Naktong Bulge was merely the latest in a series of severe trials it had undergone since its arrival in Korea on in the first week July. The first U.S. Army Division to be sent from Japan, it was also (arguably) the least prepared for combat. Committed to battle almost immediately after debarking in Korea, it nearly lost its leading element, Task Force Smith, in the vicinity of Osan on the opposite side of the peninsula. In the week that followed, it fought a series of costly delaying actions before withdrawing behind the Kum River. By then it had suffered forty-five hundred casualties. But its ordeals had not yet ended. At the Kum River North Korean forces turned its flanks, capturing some artillery, then routed it at Taejon, this time capturing its commanding general, Major General William F. Dean. By the time it straggled across the Naktong

River on 3 August, the division retained very little fighting effectiveness. The casualties suffered by the 24th Infantry Division constituted more than half of the cumulative losses of the Eighth Army through 15 August.[4]

Having spent a single day out of action and in army reserve, the division and its new commander, Major General John H. Church, hoped that the Naktong position would provide respite from the travails of July. They had good reason for believing that this would be the case. For the first time friendly forces occupied positions on the division's flanks and reinforcements, as well as replacements and supplies for its own depleted units, flowed from the rear unimpeded. As well, the sector was relatively quiet, with the river providing what seemed a strong barrier against enemy attacks.

But the river's protection was illusory. Although it was over eleven hundred feet wide, it normally ranged only one to three meters in depth, and fell to very low levels in late summer—no more than a foot deep in some places. Thus it was fordable in several locations; only its steep banks hindered crossing by vehicles. Almost amazingly, the division's defense scheme called for the weak occupation of the river frontage by separated platoons of infantry, with the parent battalion dug in on high ground several miles to the rear. Overall, the division defended with two of its three infantry regiments forward and one in reserve. Each regiment in turn had only two battalions of infantry. The two forward regiments, the 21st and 34th, each kept their second battalion another four miles to the rear in a reserve position, suitably placed (or so it was thought) for responding to attacks on outposts manned by its sister battalion. The 19th Infantry, in overall division reserve, deployed a battalion in each forward regiment's zone another four or five miles back. The division command post stood even farther to the rear, at Changnyong, over a dozen miles from the river's edge.

Night patrols and day observation supposedly filled the gaps between the platoon outposts on the banks of the Naktong, and the command posts of the regiments and division, rearward of their reserve formations, relied upon wire communications for tactical command and control of this defensive scheme. Given the proven weaknesses of the Eighth Army to date in patrolling and counterattacking, this deployment remained an open invitation for North Korean infiltration and penetration attacks. Although the division defended a frontage of only sixteen air miles, the meandering river offered an actual thirty-four miles of frontage to be somehow covered. And this at a time when the division reported its overall effectiveness at 53 percent with grave shortages in infantrymen, artillery, engineers, mortars, tanks, recoilless rifles, and ammunition.[5]

Facing the 24th Division, the North Korean 4th Infantry Division probably numbered just over seven thousand troops and had only twelve artillery pieces left in action. The division had performed well in the taking of Seoul and had overrun Task Force Smith in early July, and had then pressured and pursued the 24th Infantry Division to the Naktong River. It therefore "knew" the 24th Division well and continued to hold the initiative over it.[6]

After scouting the Naktong and the lines of the 24th Division for two days, including crossing the river at several points with patrols, the North Korean 4th Division attacked around midnight of 6 August. Wading or using rafts to cross the river, North Korean assault elements achieved complete surprise, falling upon the 34th Infantry positions in the Bulge with overwhelming strength. The first indication to American commanders of any problems at the river's edge came with the appearance of the defeated battalion commander in the command post of the regiment's reserve battalion commander at 0330. The 21st Infantry fared better in its sector, on the river north of the Bulge, because the 34th Infantry had borne the brunt of the North Korean attack.

The 24th Division launched several counterattacks, but could not prevent the North Koreans from driving into the Bulge and establishing a bridgehead containing two of the North Korean 4th Division's three regiments and measuring four by five miles. Having engaged all of the regiments of the U.S. 24th Division, the enemy was now able to his use floating and underwater bridges to move reinforcements into the bridgehead without further interference.

The North Koreans resumed their attacks on 10 August, pushing the Americans back and attempting a turning maneuver from the south preparatory to enveloping the entire division. All three regiments stood dangerously overextended and depleted. The division reported itself 40 percent effective and the 34th Infantry, mustering barely eleven hundred men, reported 24 percent effectiveness. The North Koreans had largely driven the 34th Infantry from its defensive zone, and the Eighth Army, belatedly grasping the extent of the unfolding crisis, committed its reserve to the fighting. Previously, the Eighth Army had thought the 24th Division faced infiltration in regimental strength or less, and had characterized combat as light as late as the evening of 9 August. At this point the 27th Infantry—now back with 25th Division—was ordered to move a reinforced battalion three thousand yards into the 24th Division's zone from the south to counter the enemy penetration. Additionally, the remaining Eighth Army operational reserve, comprising Colonel John G. Hill's 9th Infantry Regiment (vanguard of the 2nd Infantry Division, still offloading from the U.S. at Pusan), was ordered to reinforce the 24th Division, less one battalion held back by General Walker under army control. Sadly, the strangely ineffectual Major General Church ordered the 9th Infantry into a frontal counterattack with too little preparation and it simply merged into the confused mass of units. As if to make amends for his mistake, Church placed Colonel Hill in command of a task force comprising the 19th and 34th Infantry Regiments and a battalion of the 21st Infantry, ordering a counterattack on the eleventh. Neither Church nor his assistant division commander took tactical direction of the fight.

While the Americans scrambled to halt the enemy advance, the North Korean 4th Division continued attacking through the night with the two regiments it had gotten across the river. The North Koreans pushed into the undefended southern flank of the Americans, who now would have to fight for their main supply route between Yongsan and Kyungyo, which the North Koreans cut at several points on 12 August.[7]

General Walker, aware that Eighth Army's position was unraveling, ordered the entire 27th Infantry and a battalion of the 23rd Infantry (2nd Infantry Division) into the combat zone. Attacking on 13 August, the 1st Battalion, 23rd Infantry restored the main supply route while the 27th Infantry cleared the 24th Division's open southern flank of enemy troops. This improved situation allowed Task Force Hill to repulse North Korean attacks all along the front lines that night and to launch another counterattack on the fourteenth. Rain fell that morning, ruining the coordination of air and artillery support with the infantry attacks, which proved ragged and weak in execution through the end of the day. The North Korean 4th Division undoubtedly suffered heavy casualties but its troops held their ground and inflicted casualties on the 24th Division assault troops that the latter could ill afford.

An unwelcome surprise came in the first appearance of T-34 tanks in the Naktong Bulge, in front of positions held by the 19th Infantry. The Americans called for air and artillery strikes, but to no avail. At 1800 a tank accompanied by infantry crashed into the lines of its 1st Battalion, causing it to retreat south into the 9th Infantry's sector, bringing the day's counterattack to an ignominious end. The North Koreans attacked again that night, and at 0300 four T-34s broke into the lines of the 2nd Battalion, 9th Infantry at Turok. After stopping briefly to shoot up company supply dumps the tanks rumbled off into the darkness, evidently without any clear sense of direction. At dawn, they remained inside U.S. lines but short of the vital supply dumps near Yongsan. An intrepid rifleman—Corporal Robert C. Carroll of H Company—singlehandedly attacked the intruders, disabling one tank with a 3.5 inch rocket launcher shot and then finishing it off by pouring gasoline over its engine cover. The other three tanks promptly fled the scene.[8]

General Church doggedly ordered yet another counterattack for 15 August, and it met with the same lack of success as his previous efforts. The 27th Infantry had returned to its parent division to the south and the 1st Battalion, 23rd Infantry continued to cover the main supply route, but Church's division had been unable to defeat the 4th North Korean Division or recover the ground lost after ten days of action. It was at this point that General Walker decided to assign another one of his scarce reserve units to the battle, the 1st Provisional Marine Brigade.

Visiting the 24th Division rear command post at Miryang on the morning of 15 August, Walker told Church, "I am going to give you the marine brigade. I want this situation cleared up, and quick!" This comment can be found in official histories and other accounts of the brigade's actions in Korea—which, however, seldom make any mention whatsoever of the other "fire brigade" units that had already been sent to help the badly battered 24th Division. Nor do most accounts explain that Walker spoke impulsively in this instance, and that he confirmed the order only later in the day, after conferring with his staff at Eighth Army Headquarters in Taegu. The operational directive issued to General Church that day ordered him to use the division, the marine brigade, and a tank platoon from the 23rd Infantry to drive the enemy back across the Naktong, commencing 17 August.[9]

Marines into the Bulge: Naktong I

The marine brigade had broken off its counterattack with Task Force Kean on 12 August and had withdrawn the next day, with Taplett's 3rd Battalion, 5th Marines remaining for an additional day to protect the marine corps artillery left in the rear of RCT 5, following the Bloody Gulch debacle. The marines' movement out of the 25th Division sector to the old assembly area at Changwon began the morning of 14 August, but General Craig instead received orders at 0130 to move on to Miryang and prepare for operations with the 24th Division. By this time, he understood that the enemy had achieved a breakthrough in that area. He rode from Masan in a train with his troops of 2nd Battalion, 5th Marines, reaching Miryang at 0330 on the fifteenth. The remainder of the troops arrived later in the day. Using his helicopter, he met with General Church and his staff in the afternoon, returning to brief his staff and unit commanders at 1900 (the 5th Marines' 1st and 3rd Battalions remained en route on their trains, arriving at 2000 and 2115 respectively). The commander of the 1st Battalion, 11th Marines noted that they enjoyed "their first hot meal and satisfactory rest period since starting the operation."[10]

Elsewhere, the general crisis continued to build for the Eighth Army. The 27th Infantry moved to its blocking position fight in the Bowling Alley north of Taegu, along with a battalion of the 23rd Infantry. The air force flew 260 ground-support sorties on August 15: 110 for the ROK divisions, 68 for the 1st Cavalry Division, 43 for the 24th Infantry Division, and 29 for the 25th Division.[11]

The 24th Infantry Division went over to the defensive while the marine brigade arrived and assembled at Miryang. Despite mounting losses the North Korean 4th Division continued to attack, conducting daylight "human wave" charges against the 9th, 19th, and 34th Infantry Regiments. Although the weakest regiment, the 34th Infantry, was forced back from its positions, the 9th and 19th weathered the attacks well—an indication that the 4th Division was reaching the end of its tether, suffering in particular from the U.S. artillery fire now concentrated upon it.

Having dissolved Task Force Hill, General Church now presided over the counterattack planned for 17 August. All the regiments would take part in the attack, with the most pressure thrown against the North Korean positions by the marines on the southern flank and

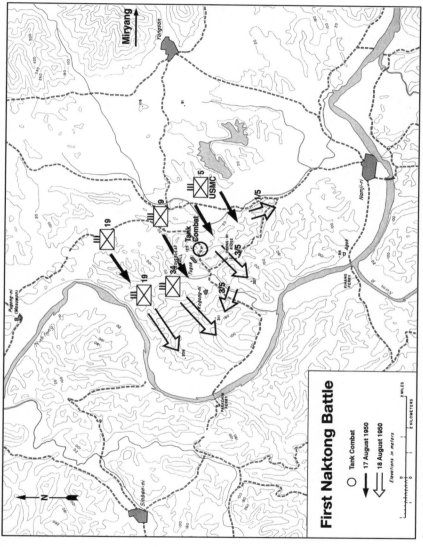

Army Map Service, printed in Appleman, *South to the Naktong, North to the Yalu: June–November, 1950.* Modified by W. Stephen Hill.

the 19th Infantry, pressing from the north, moving along the left bank of the Naktong. The 9th Infantry would attack in the center, north of the main supply route to take Tugok village and the ridge mass behind it, while the 5th Marines, operating south of the road, would take Obong village and the long ridgeline of the same name running southeast toward the southern bend of the Naktong River and the Bulge. The 5th Marines would then continue westward across two more ridges to clear the southern half of the enemy bridgehead. The 19th Infantry, with support from the 34th on its left, had a similar mission to clear three hill masses and occupy the northern half of the Bulge.[12]

Complexities mounted at a time when the outcome of combat actions favored the simplest plan. The timely movement of the 5th Marines into the lines of the 24th Division took on key importance, as it would relieve the 34th Infantry for its employment in the northern advance. In addition, General Church had insisted that the marine brigade secure the refused southern flank that covered the main supply route leading to the rear, which had proven vulnerable several times in the last ten days of action.

Craig had agreed to the army plan but had requested no fewer than 144 trucks to provide rapid movement from the Miryang assembly area into the 24th Division's positions. Inexplicably, the division provided only forty-three trucks, and these arrived three hours behind schedule. The division managed to locate another twenty-nine trucks, still insufficient for the marine brigade's transportation needs. The 24th Infantry Division had once again failed to carry out its assigned task.[13]

Taplett's 3rd Battalion arrived first, relieving the 34th Infantry at 0400 of its flank guard duties; but the leading assault battalion, Roise's 2nd Battalion, had to march most of the way from Yongsan, where the marines de-trucked, in order to relieve a company of the 9th Infantry on the south side of the main supply route. Trucks did not arrive at Miryang for Newton's 1st Battalion until 0615, and it took most of the morning to move up. Only one battalion at a time would go into action. On 16 August, Lieutenant Colonel Murray reconnoitered the enemy positions to his regiment's front and decided that, since he only had two companies per battalion, and to ensure that he had enough strength "to last this thing out," he would attack in column of battalions. Later, he noted, "some people asked me why I didn't try to flank the enemy. Well . . . there really wasn't a flank. They were on a long ridgeline. So, I attacked in a column of battalions and I had coordinated with the army unit next to us.[14]

Murray had apparently judged the 9th Infantry as rather weak and under strength and also noted that Colonel Hill's objective, Cloverleaf Hill, lay some distance farther west than the nearest peaks of Obong Ridge. He therefore proposed that the two regiments not attack simultaneously, as ordered by 24th Division, but in sequence, with the 9th Infantry supporting the 5th Marines by fire as the latter took their high ground, whence the marines would cover the advance of Hill's troops. Hill agreed and apparently passed the word to Church, who accepted the decision of his frontline commanders.[15]

The North Korean 4th Infantry Division had by this time likely shot its bolt. After days of attacks into the 24th Infantry Division lines, the strength of the North Korean infantry regiments had fallen drastically. Rations and ammunition were nearly exhausted, and the extensive use of captured U.S. machine guns and other weapons indicated some of the division's material shortcomings. Replacements were deserting in significant numbers, but the surviving small-unit leaders remained tenacious and were able to mount a spirited resistance to the American attack on 17 August.

The preparatory fires began at 0730. The artillery of 1st Battalion, 11th Marines fired for ten minutes, then checked firing to allow an impressive mass attack by eighteen MAG-33 Corsairs. Many observers, including General Craig, thought it a magnificent demonstration of marine corps close air support, but it seems to have made little impact on the North Korean defenders dug in on the reverse slope (opposite the hillside the Americans would climb). By then, the North Koreans had been on the receiving end of U.S. air attacks almost daily for over a month, and had adapted well to the circumstances by digging in deeply and keeping their heads down when the Corsairs appeared. In the estimation of the men who would conduct the ground attack (2nd Battalion, 5th Marines), the air strikes ended too soon, and they later faulted air support for only using a few napalm canisters. But the airmen could not use napalm effectively against ill-defined area targets, preferring to employ 1000- or 500-lb. bombs for such preparatory strikes. In all that day, the F4Us of VMF-214 and VMF-323 flew 34 and 27 sorties, expending 1000-lb. bombs in the initial strike, following up with 500-lb. bombs, and finally strafing the enemy with 5-inch rockets and 20mm cannons just ahead of the advancing marine riflemen.[16]

As the assaulting marines of D and E companies emerged from their attack positions and began advancing across open ground, five M26 tanks of 3rd Platoon, A Company, arrived on the scene. Halting fifty yards beyond the infantry start line, the tanks fired their 90mm cannon and .30-caliber machine guns at enemy positions on Obong Ridge. Returning fire with antitank guns and 14.5mm antitank rifles, the North Koreans scored two dozen hits but nevertheless failed to even disable any of the M26s.

The men of the rifle companies strode gamely toward the imposing hills, crossing a lateral road and filing, upright and determined, along the rice paddy dikes and bean patches. Few of them relished a frontal attack, but there was no enemy flank to exploit. As the marines began their climb a few sniper shots rang out. Then the machine guns joined in.

Despite all the artillery and air support used, Lieutenant Colonel Roise's two assault companies encountered fierce and deadly small-arms fire from each flank as they ascended the slopes of the ridge. Enemy soldiers and guns dug in behind neighboring hills in previously unobserved reverse slope positions could fire on the Americans on the front slope of Obong Ridge. From the southern part of the ridgeline, not yet subject to U.S. assault, these weapons peppered Company E, while heavy fire from Tugok village and Cloverleaf Hill flayed the ranks of D Company. As the unwounded and lightly wounded struggled uphill in the building heat of the day, North Koreans rolled or threw hand grenades by the volley down the slope.

Men fought back, sometimes against an unseen enemy, and several of them made dents in the enemy position. An acting rifle platoon leader in D Company, Staff Sergeant T. Albert Crowson, came to the aid of one of his squads pinned down among the rocks. He single-handedly scouted out two offending machine-gun positions, then stood up and fired his semi-automatic carbine so fast and true that he killed four and wounded others, silencing the guns. Twice that morning small numbers of men reached the top of the ridge, but were driven back by energetic automatic weapons fire, incoming mortar rounds, and hand grenades. By midday it was clear that 2nd Battalion was stuck on the ridge, with too many men killed and wounded to seize and clear it. Mostly they huddled among the scrub pines, rocks, and gullies for protection, counting out their remaining ammunition.[17]

D Company had a just few men on the ridgeline crest they assaulted and the rest of them and E Company remained halfway up the slope of their objective. They had already suffered 23 killed and 119 wounded.

Lieutenant Colonel Murray and General Craig both realized the error of staggering their assault with the neighboring 9th Infantry. Calling upon Colonel Hill to commence his attack as soon as possible, Murray ordered the 1st Battalion, 5th Marines at 1245 to pass through the 2nd Battalion and carry the ridge. Receiving the order at 1330, Lieutenant Colonel Newton ordered his two assault companies forward while leading his command group to join Roise's and coordinate the passage of his lines. The tank platoon shifted its support to the follow-on battalion. The tanks would cycle by two-tank sections to the rear four times that day to replenish their ammunition stocks. Hill launched his 9th Infantry attack at 1300, sending his 2nd Battalion through Tugok while 24th Division artillery pounded the battalion's assigned objective of Cloverleaf Hill. The battalion's two assault companies continued up the hill and attacked repeatedly to seize a slender foothold on Cloverleaf's ridges, from which the enemy now withdrew entirely. Although it took all afternoon, the 9th Infantry achieved its objective.

Everything depended now on the attack of 1st Battalion, 5th Marines. The riflemen of A and B Companies passed through their sister battalion at 1600, taking up the attack on their own. The fresh assault by these two companies, the continuing air and artillery bombardment, and the actions of the 9th Infantry on the Marines' right flank undoubtedly contributed to the operation's overall success. A and B Companies went up the hill through E and D companies on the left and right, respectively. Second Lieutenant Thomas H. Johnston's 2nd Platoon on the left of his A Company clung to the ground while machine-gun fire from the top of their objective hill swept over them. Moving forward through his men, he collected hand grenades. He then ascended to the crest of the hill and threw a grenade that silenced the enemy position, but he himself was caught and killed in a volley of North Korean grenades. Although A Company was held up as well by flanking fire from the south, B Company crested the ridge shortly after 1700 and turned left to clear two peaks, digging in at 2000 and bringing up their machine guns to punish the fleeing enemy. A Company retained a perilous hold on the slope. Captain Ike Fenton, who had started the day as the B Company second-in-command, was the only officer left unwounded in his unit. His men had managed to work around the northern flank of the enemy once artillery and mortar fire had suppressed most of the enemy fire from Turok. In the last light of the day, A and B Companies dug in on the left slope and right crest of their objectives and awaited the enemy's move.[18]

Unbeknownst to the bruised and bloodied riflemen of the 1st and 2nd Battalions, 5th Marines, the day's effort had almost broken the North Korean 4th Division. Attacking later than the 24th Division plan specified, the 19th and 34th Infantry had also taken their assigned hill in the afternoon, thus pressing the enemy farther back into the Naktong Bulge. In desperate straits, the North Koreans threw what they had back into the fight that very evening.

The North Korean 4th Division struggled to hold its collapsing position, even as it began to withdraw across the Naktong. What could have been devastating attacks on the 5th Marines' left flank and 9th Infantry positions on Cloverleaf instead became limited-objective attacks that were not pressed with the customary North Korean tenacity. The first attack to hit the U.S. lines came at twilight attack along the Naktong-Yongson main road dividing the army and marine units. Four T-34 tanks followed by infantry moved between the newly occupied peaks of Obong and Cloverleaf and headed up onto Observation Hill, the last high ground before Yongsan, where the 24th Infantry Division's headquarters was located. Some air force F-51 fighters made a few strafing passes on the tanks, but to no effect, and were called off by air controllers in order to avoid hitting friendly troops. On the north side of the road, the 5th Marines antitank company set up its 75mm recoilless rifles; on the other side, assault men of the 1st Battalion, 5th Marines armed with 3.5-inch rocket launchers scrambled to set up firing positions.

The tankers of First Lieutenant Granville G. Sweet's 3rd Platoon had supported the 5th Marine attacks all day, and had then moved to the rear of the battalion command posts to refuel, rearm, and perform maintenance on their vehicles. Alerted by radio from B Company's Captain Fenton of the approach of enemy tanks, Sweet ordered his men to move out as soon as they could clear their vehicles for action. So anxious were the tankers to go forward that they did not even replace some of the caps on their fuel tanks, stopping only to commandeer and move aside several trucks and jeeps parked in their way. Moving past the vital medical, supply, and command post positions of the battalions, they stopped in a narrow defile one hundred yards short of a turn in the road to make their stand. There was only room for three M26 tanks abreast, so Sweet moved his tank behind tanks A-32, A-33 and, A-34 to observe and direct the action from his vehicle. The tanks were packed together so tightly that the 90mm muzzle blast from the center tank set fire to spilled gasoline on the engine cover of the right tank, but then extinguished the flames with the concussion of the next round.

The combined effects of tank and antitank weapons devastated the three leading enemy tanks, as General Craig reported to the army chain of command a week later:

Enemy tanks were moving northwest along road toward our position. . . . The enemy tanks fired approximately four rounds of HE ammunition at our troops without results. The enemy came under fire of our tanks, 75mm recoilless rifles and 3.5″ rocket launchers almost simultaneously. Three M-26 tanks moved 900 yards southwest down the road and positioned themselves overlooking a curve in the road. Two of our tanks were abreast and opened fire at a range of 100 yards as the first two enemy tanks came around the curve in the road.

The first M-26 fired two rounds of APC [armor piercing, capped; a conventional solid shot round] ammunition at each of the enemy tanks, a total of six rounds. All rounds fired at the hull penetrated the enemy armor.

The second M-26 fired one round of APC at the first enemy tank, one round of HVAP [high velocity armor piercing] and two APC at the second tank and four rounds of HE ammunition at the third enemy tank. Our second tank fired the HE ammunition through a penetration made previously by APC ammunition through the machine gun bow mount, front slope plate of the third enemy tank. . . .

No Marine aircraft participated in the attack on the enemy tanks since the Tactical Air Coordinator (airborne) called planes off to prevent endangering our troops.[19]

The fourth enemy tank turned and fled the carnage, eventually falling victim to an army rocket launcher team from A Company, 9th Infantry. The North Korean infantry faded away without taking part in the action. The three North Korean T-34s destroyed by 3rd platoon were the war's first tank-versus-tank "kills" by the M26.[20]

After nightfall, more deadly North Korean infantry assaults fell upon the men of the 1st Battalion, 5th Marines up on the ridgeline. Beginning at 0230 against them and at 0355 against the 9th Infantry, the assaulting enemy soldiers threw grenades and charged the American position with their submachine guns blazing. B Company of the 1st Battalion, 5th Marines fought them off in about forty-five minutes, and A Company, 9th Infantry yielded one hundred yards on Cloverleaf Hill but then held firm through the night. Unfortunately, the North Korean assault hit the distended lines of the 1st Battalion's A Company, with the momentum of a downhill charge broking the center platoon and forcing the company commander, Captain John R. Stevens, to pull back. This move exposed the 5th Marines' left flank to attack, but the North Koreans did not press their advantage, instead withdrawing over the hilltops of Obong Ridge, pounded by marine artillery and mortar fire.

In the early morning hours of 18 August the much-diminished strength of the North Korean 4th Division became readily apparent to the marines of A Company as they scrambled to the top of Obong Ridge beginning at 0700. Only a few scattered enemy troops remained in the area. Second Lieutenant Frank Muetzel, who led the machine guns of A Company, started the day by receiving a random bullet wound to his leg. Limping to the top with the rest of the ninety or so men left in his company, he found countless North Korean bodies intermixed with the bodies of marines from A and G Companies. After the wounded were taken away, only the dead remained, the stench already rising with the sun. Muetzel took charge of the 2nd Platoon, replacing his tentmate Second Lieutenant Thomas A. Johnston, and ordered his men to dig in.[21]

Major Lund then led the first flight of VMF-323 Corsairs over the battle zone, personally dropping three 500-lb. bombs and firing sixteen rockets at enemy positions and other targets of opportunity. About ninety men remained in action in A Company, and these now joined with about as many men from B Company to sweep the ridgeline to the south, taking four more peaks against token North Korean resistance. The 5th Marines were now the masters of Obong Ridge along its entire length.

In the meantime, Lieutenant Colonel Murray had ordered the 3rd Battalion, 5th Marines forward for the assault on the regiment's next objective, Hill 207. He and his staff thought that Hill 207 anchored the main line of resistance of the North Korean 4th Division. However, the enemy instead had held the forward ridges of Obong, Cloverleaf, and Ohang Hill (in the 19th Infantry zone). Badly beaten and in even worse shape in terms of strength and supplies, the North Korean survivors now streamed for the river, although some pockets of resistance remained to be taken. For this task in the 5th Marines' zone, Lieutenant Colonel Taplett's 3rd Battalion proved more than adequate.

Once again, the seasoned 3rd Tank Platoon supported the marine assault, firing from positions on the main supply route just a half-mile west of the site of the previous night's tank engagement. In addition, Lieutenant Pomeroy's 1st Tank Platoon covered the advance of 1st Battalion, 5th Marines along the peaks and saddles of the Obong Ridge. With artillery, mortars, and aircraft pounding Hill 207, Taplett's Companies G and H jumped off in column at 1000, with H Company leading and veering toward the left (western) spur and G Company heading to the right. When a group of enemy defenders tried to flank H Company, it came in view of Lieutenant Sweet's tank platoon and was cut down by cannon and machine guns firing at a range of just three hundred yards. Hill 207 fell quickly to Taplett's rifle companies and the supporting arms and tank fire shifted to the final objective, Hill 311, lying to the west across the main road.

At this point, approximately 1230, the marines on Hill 207 and Obong Ridge spotted the enemy retreating in plain view toward the river. The complete array of the brigade's direct and indirect fire weapons flayed the enemy, as the Corsair pilots of VMF-214 added even more ordnance, returning to strafe after completing their assigned close support missions, covering both shores of the river. So complete was the rout of the North Korean 4th Division that the 3rd Platoon tanks were used to mount riflemen of G Company to move them to the base of Hill 311 for the next attack. Meanwhile, the 1st Platoon of tanks had arrived to take up the fire support tasks and 3rd Battalion, 5th Marines attacked Hill 311, commencing at 1545. Attacking up parallel spurs again, G Company gained a foothold on the summit, while H Company encountered a tough pocket of resistance on the right spur. The company commander, Captain Joseph Feagan, was seriously wounded in the action, and the advance was halted until morning, the riflemen digging in for the night. In the late afternoon, 2nd Battalion, 5th Marines settled into the newly seized positions on Hill 207. The brigade had thus taken all three of its objectives at the same time that the 19th and 34th Infantry did the same on the northern flank of the Naktong Bulge. The next day would bring them together facing what was now the funeral pyre of the North Korean 4th Division.

The Corsair pilots logged in a great day of close support and opportune strikes on 18 August, with each squadron flying forty-three sorties to drop dozens of bombs and fire hundreds of rockets. The artillery of 1st Battalion, 11th Marines continued firing what would total 4,390 rounds of 105mm in the 110 missions called for in the three-day battle. Seldom mentioned by marine corps sources were the sorties flown by air force fighter-bombers in support of the Eighth Army. For the 17–19 August period these totaled 773 sorties: 206 (26 for the 24th Division), 336, and 231 (17 for the 24th Division). General Craig's mention of F-51 missions in front of the brigade indicated their support of marine forces in this battle, as had happened earlier with Task Force Kean.[22]

Dawn on the 19 August brought swift action by the 5th Marines as they and the soldiers of the 24th Infantry Division collapsed the Naktong Pocket. The riflemen of 3rd Battalion, 5th Marines swept over the remainder of the crest of Hill 311 and, finding it deserted, occupied positions at 0645 on the slope facing the Naktong River and the last fleeing troops of the enemy. Contact made with the 34th Infantry completed the operation that morning. Lieutenant Colonel Murray then ordered his battalions to hold their positions for eventual relief by the army, in the meantime sending patrols to the near bank of the Naktong to complete the sweep of the zone. A few mortar volleys were exchanged with the enemy, but the fight was over. Large amounts of enemy materiel left in the zone demonstrated that the North Korean 4th Division had lost all of its major equipment; and the army later reported burying about twelve hundred enemy dead. Between 1600 and 2030, the 19th Infantry relieved the 5th Marines in their positions, and that night the marines were trucked to the rear over roads churned by a fortnight of battle, arriving at Yongsan the next morning. From

Yongsan, additional trucks took the 5th Marines to the rail station at Miryang. The brigade then retraced its rail and road movement of the prior week back to Masan and a new bivouac area. The cost to the brigade of retaking its portion of the Naktong Bulge tallied 66 men killed, one missing, and 278 wounded.[23]

After the marine brigade returned to Eighth Army reserve, the 24th Infantry Division also came out of the lines, relieved by the 2nd Infantry Division, and finally entered reserve after fifty-five days of near-continuous combat. There really was no comparison between the two organizations as each faced the needed rest, refit, and rehabilitation. The marines had lost little equipment and rated at around 80 percent effectiveness in the army system. The 24th Infantry Division rated itself about 43 percent effective, and would soon disband the 34th Infantry Regiment in order to rebuild its other two infantry regiments. As for the North Korean 4th Infantry Division, it would not reform for several months, after the Chinese intervention in the Korean War. Ironically, as its survivors streamed across the Naktong in search of safety, North Korean headquarters published the order naming it a guards division for its actions at Taejon.[24]

The combat units of the marine brigade had encountered a far more difficult task at the Naktong Bulge than had been the case over a week prior with Task Force Kean. Instead of pushing forward in a secondary attack against a weak, delaying opponent as in the Sachon attack, the men of 5th Marines had to fight their way up a hill mass against determined resistance from a fanatical foe that knew how to dig in against U.S. artillery and air support. Attacking in sequence, with only two assault companies at a time, the marines had done all that could have been expected of them in dangerous and lethal circumstances, but had not carried the enemy positions as planned.

This had also been the case for 2nd and 3rd Battalions of the 5th Marines when they had separately attacked the North Koreans in the hills surrounding Chingdong on 8 and 9 August. Against Obong Ridge, two battalions in sequence struggled to take the enemy positions on the 17 August, and the job had to be completed the next day. The events of the eighteenth progressed far better, but one wonders if the initial attacks had been too hasty, approaching over open ground with no smoke screen and supporting direct fires, and with insufficient fire support. All seemed as if the enemy had been underestimated. Lieutenant Colonel Murray had suspected that Obong Ridge was not the main line of resistance. If he had known how well defended it was, would he have attacked with two rifle companies of a single battalion, preceded by only ten minutes of artillery fire and a single strike by fighter-bombers? Even the tank support on the second day seems to have been much more effective than the artillery and air support used against the enemy.

Had the brigade's ground combat power thus far been effectively employed in the campaign? Almost every aspect of the arrival and attack of the brigade during 16–17 August revealed a rushed and poorly coordinated action. Yet General Church had asked for an even more precipitous attack on the evening of 16 August. The decision by Colonel Murray to attack alone after halting the 9th Infantry's movement forward on the marines' right flank seems in retrospect to have been badly conceived. Subsequently, marine corps leaders would criticize the army for letting the marines carry the bulk of the mission against the Naktong Bulge, but the choices of tactics and execution seem to have remained with the brigade and 5th Marines alone. The 24th Infantry Division had called for tactically unimaginative frontal attacks along each side of the main supply route, and the 5th Marines had simply complied.

Whenever the North Koreans had attacked on the road, they were butchered and usually thrown back by U.S. defensive fires. Only movements and attacks made off road by the enemy had succeeded. Here one would note that the weaker 19th and 34th Infantry Regiments, although weaker than their marine counterparts, had succeeded in their cross-country attacks in the northern zone of the Bulge, where their efforts in the center of the Bulge days earlier had not gained any significant ground against the North Korean 4th Division. Perhaps, in the end, it was the freshness and fighting spirit of the 5th Marines that had carried the day, making a difference unmatched by other organizations that had been ground steadily down in almost continuous fighting during July and August. The casualty toll would support such a finding: on 17 August, the 9th Infantry took 73 casualties, the 19th Infantry only 10. The same day, a single battalion, the 2nd Battalion, 5th Marines, had suffered 142 casualties (including 23 dead), falling out of action by 1600. When the North Koreans abandoned Obong Ridge, they left behind forty-three heavy and light machine guns. In the circumstances, and absent any tactical advantage, flesh and blood could only do so much.[25]

In contrast, the employment of marine aviation in support of the ground troops of the brigade had functioned well and with the effectiveness anticipated in its doctrine and peacetime training. This success took on paramount importance to senior marine officers, not only providing proof of aviation's combat effectiveness, but also to highlight the doctrine of air-ground cooperation as it had evolved in the postwar marine corps.

Ironically, the very success of marine airmen in August ignited anew some hard feelings generated by the interservice competition at the time of the defense reforms of the postwar years. Such sensitivity was never far from the minds of service leaders, as evidenced in a typical message sent from General Shepherd to General Cates when the brigade began its initial moves to the Naktong:

> Reports from Korea indicate that limited number of small helicopters available there are proving of great usefulness in reconnaissance of difficult mountain terrain which exhausts flank patrols. Further consider that were troop carrying type available they would increase greatly the ability of troops to advance rapidly . . . from one key terrain locality to the next. Accordingly recommend deployment of maximum available helicopter force [to] FECOM [Far East Command] earliest. *Consider this unequalled opportunity to make significant contribution while at the same time demonstrating marine foresight and initiative.*[Emphasis added][26]

But Shepherd underestimated the repercussions of such marine corps success, regardless of "foresight and initiative," and MacArthur's senior air force commander took frequent umbrage at what he regarded as excessive publicity for the exploits of marine corps aviation.

Lieutenant General Stratemeyer complained vigorously in August to MacArthur and his own air force chain of command about media accounts written from the escort carriers that operated the two marine corps fighter squadrons. Stratemeyer charged that articles published during 14–23 August likely were coached and prewritten by navy and marine corps officers to further their ends in a continuation of the defense reorganization fight of 1946–48. "I am completely convinced," he asserted, "as I have said in both my messages quoted above, that the carefully planned campaign is designed to do two things: (a) discredit the Air Force, and (b) unjustifiably enhance the prestige of the United States Marines at the expense of both the Army and the Air Force.[27]

On August 16, Stratemeyer sent a stern letter to General Walker, further venting his ire.[28] But Walker, preoccupied by his fight against North Korean forces, did not rise to the bait, replying in part on August 18:

> Without the slightest intent of disparaging the support of the Air Forces, I must say that I, in common with the vast majority of officers of the Army, feel strongly that the Marine system of close air support has much to commend it. Marine aviation is designed, equipped and trained for the sole purpose of supporting Marine ground forces. It operates equally well from land bases or carriers, often permitting support from short distances not possible if there is sole dependence upon land air bases. During training and maneuvers, Marine aviation works constantly with ground units to perfect the communications and coordination so essential in the application of any type of supporting fires, whether delivered by aircraft, artillery, or supporting infantry weapons. Tactical air support parties are available to units down to and including the infantry battalion. In short, although there are probably strong reasons such as governmental economy to the contrary, I feel strongly that the Army would be well advised to emulate the Marine Corps and have its own tactical support aviation.[29]

Walker's supportive stance for marine corps aviation deeply disappointed Stratemeyer. General Craig could just as easily have written Walker's letter, so well did it represent marine corps aviation doctrine. Paradoxically, navy and marine leaders delivered the satisfaction Stratemeyer apparently sought. Admiral Sherman condemned the publication of such articles and Brigadier General Cushman answered diplomatically:

> The cooperation and assistance rendered this command by both the U.S. Air Force and Army in becoming established in Japan has been splendid. Without this whole-hearted support, our units could not have been deployed into action as rapidly as they were. I have the highest regard and admiration for the work the U.S. Air Force and Army are doing and have done

in the past. To insure speedy and successful termination of hostilities it is mandatory that the armed services continue to maintain close and harmonious relations.[30]

Still smarting, Stratemeyer sarcastically advised Washington on 26 August that air force chief of staff General Hoyt Vandenberg "ought to throw out the idea that perhaps there should be an increase of Marine divisions and a cut in divisions of the Army."[31]

Reserve and Redeployment Preparations

When the ground troops of the marine brigade returned to Changwon, they assembled three miles southwest of the village in a new bivouac area closer to Masan, where they would rest and prepare to rejoin the 1st Marine Division at sea for the September 15 amphibious landing at Inchon. A typical expanse of rural farmland, the Masan fields quickly became known in marine corps lore as the "Bean Patch." It would again host the 5th Marines and the rest of the 1st Marine Division before the end of the year.

While at the Bean Patch, the marines rested and recuperated, showered and swam in a nearby river, cleaned and repaired weapons and vehicles, and conducted routine training, chiefly in the form of patrolling. Most of their personal belongings had disappeared with their packs, dropped off at the piers upon arrival, never to be seen again. Replacement weapons, web gear, boots, and uniforms also remained scarce. Tents had to be improvised from any material at hand, including spare dungaree uniforms or field jackets strung on bamboo supports.

Starting on 26 August, the battalions practiced platoon and company tactics, drilled on their crew-served weapons, and conducted route marches. These activities irritated the men somewhat, but were needed in order to incorporate replacements just then joining the brigade from marine corps posts and stations in the United States. Not surprisingly, Captain Fenton found very few combat veterans among the replacements, most of whom had been performing guard duty or administrative jobs and who had to be schooled in tactics and handling weapons that they would need in only days, not the weeks contemplated.[32]

Because of its operational reserve status in the rear of the 25th Infantry Division, General Craig and Lieutenant Colonel Murray reunited with the division's commanders and staff sections to plan counterattack and reinforcement missions in the event that they were called upon to assist. Accordingly, the 1st Battalion, 11th Marines reported to the 25th Division artillery commander on 23 August, and was assigned to support RCT 5 and reinforce the reformed 555th Field Artillery Battalion. Returning to Chingdong and its old firing positions, the marines fired 2,413 rounds on 130 missions through 31 August. Although frequently under counterbattery fire, the battalion reported no serious casualties.[33]

Planning continued for the employment with the 1st Marine Division at Inchon, but Craig noted on 30 August that the information his officers brought from Tokyo meetings demonstrated that there was "much left to be resolved and plans [were] very sketchy." Fortunately, the replacement pool ordered by the commandant on 14 July had been accelerated enough to deliver some three hundred men to Masan during this vital period. Combined with men returned from the field hospitals and some volunteers for infantry duty taken in from its own support units, the brigade accomplished its recovery at Masan—and not a day too soon.[34]

Once Again into the Breach: Naktong II

Throughout the perilous days of August and September, the Eighth Army continued to be pressed by an enemy now seriously weakened by losses and deficient in all military requirements except for ideological fervor. Almost incredibly, the North Korean command ordered yet another all-out offensive that once again imperiled Eighth Army's survival. Using up to 60 percent conscripts from South Korea, most without training and many without weapons, the divisions so badly battered in August rebuilt to a strength of between five thousand and ten thousand troops, each. The North Korean high command brought two new armored brigades south from Pyongyang with eighty-three newly received Soviet T-34 tanks and even managed to add two infantry divisions built from rear-area security units to its order of battle. With enemy forces thus strengthened, the Eighth Army would experience its severest crisis in the North Korean offensive of early September, at the same time the marine brigade was preparing to leave Pusan.[35]

The staged offensive began on 27 August in the Eighth Army lines' northernmost sector, which was defended by two South Korean divisions, when two North Korean divisions advanced on Pohang port and its Yonil Airfield. The main effort, however, came on 2 September, when two North Korean divisions advanced into the corridor east of Taegu, defended by two more South Korean divisions, and three more North Korean divisions approached Taegu directly, engaging the U.S. 1st Cavalry Division and a South Korean division.

In the center, on the old Naktong Bulge battlefield, The North Korean 2nd, 4th, 9th, and 10th Divisions attacked the U.S. 2nd Infantry Division and advanced on both Changnyong and Yongsan in order to cut the Taegu-Pusan road and rail connections. If success-ful, their attacks might have cut the Pusan Perimeter in two or even collapsed it.

Finally, in the south, two North Korean divisions attacked the U.S. 25th Infantry Division to drive on Masan and Pusan. The enemy timed his efforts well: the two major northern assaults were delayed until 2 September in hopes that their comrades to the south, attacking four days earlier on 29 August, would draw off U.N. forces from the eastern coastal corridor.

This final general offensive against the Eighth Army and the U.N. position at Pusan would produce the greatest casualties of the Korean War to date and far outweighed the scale of the previous efforts. At the time that MacArthur's command busily planned the amphibious riposte at Inchon and the concomitant breakout and pursuit by the Pusan Perimeter forces, the latter fought one last battle against an astonishing repeat of the enemy's "last gasp" of August. In every case, the ferocity of the enemy assaults forced U.N. troops back, and several isolated U.N. units had to fight for their very existence, all contributing by their success or sacrifice to the erosion of the enemy's offensive, gaining time for countermeasures and, where possible, the summoning of reinforcements.[36]

As the North Korean offensive unfolded and the situation became increasingly chaotic, the General Walton ordered the marine brigade to return to battle. No longer did General Craig or Lieutenant Colonel Murray study the plans for the Inchon invasion still two weeks in the future. Instead, they directed a new march by rail and road back to Miryang and the familiar assembly area from which it would reenter the Naktong battlefield.

The U.S. 2nd Infantry Division received the major blow against its positions beginning on night of 31 August. The division had taken over the former 24th Division sector as well as a considerable part of the 1st Cavalry Division lines north along the left bank of the Naktong.

The 9th Infantry Regiment stood alone in the former Naktong Bulge battlefield sector area and more, occupying over ten miles of frontage. With its two battalions of infantry and some engineer and tank support, the regiment recoiled under the assault of the North Korean 9th Division at five different crossing points. The North Koreans had infiltrated into the Bulge sector from 2130 until midnight, when the North Korean artillery dropped its preparatory barrages on the U.S. positions. While North Korean infantry pressed forward, enemy tanks crossed the river and advanced on the familiar main supply route to Yongsan. By morning, the North Koreans held both Cloverleaf and Obong Ridges, forcing the 2nd Division to fight from the inferior heights of Observation Hill and adjacent positions in order to protect Yongsan and the road leading east to Miryang and the vital interior rail and road routes.

In similar fashion, the North Korean 2nd Division attacked across the Naktong into the 23rd Infantry Regiment's positions. Also organized with only two infantry battalions, this regiment had occupied its ninemile frontage only since 29 August, and had little familiarity with its terrain. Here the North Koreans crossed at three points and drove overnight in two thrusts against Changnyong. Farther north, the North Korean 10th Division registered only slight gains against the third regiment of the 2nd Division, the 38th Infantry. Major General Lawrence B. Keiser now split his command into two parts, ordering his assistant division commander, Brigadier General Joseph S. Bradley, to direct the 9th Infantry's fight for Yongsan while he directed the rest of the division and its artillery from Changnyong.[37]

General Walker disposed of his strongest operational reserve of the entire campaign on 1 September, but he had to allocate it carefully, given the enemy's ability to threaten in every sector. The newly arrived British 27th Infantry Brigade (two infantry battalions), the marine brigade, the U.S. 27th Infantry, and the 19th Infantry all received new orders. General Craig received his instructions at around 1100 to move to Miryang and its vital road and rail center. Walker later ordered both the British brigade and the 19th Infantry to prepare for employment in the 2nd Division zone. Walker's plan at this point centered upon the marine brigade restoring the 9th Infantry lines while that regiment reestablished contact with the rest of its division to the north.[38]

Craig had alerted the 5th Marines at 0930 that day for possible action with the nearby 25th Infantry Division, which also reeled under North Korean pressure. But at 1100 he ordered the 5th Marines to move to Miryang, and Lieutenant Colonel Murray ordered his command group and 2nd Battalion into trucks and with all his other wheeled vehicles commenced his road march to Miryang, leaving the remainder of the regiment to move by train. Roise's battalion departed at 1420 and arrived first at 1800.

Four of nine trains also covered the distance that day. At 0400, 2 September, Murray ordered all his units to move to the forward assembly area already occupied by 2nd Battalion, located about four thousand yards east of Yongsan. They accomplished this movement by 1530, just in time to receive a warning order from Craig to prepare for employment in the 2nd Division's sector. Craig noted later that Eighth Army staff officers urged him to attack that afternoon, but he protested the piecemeal deployment that would amount to, emphasizing that he had not yet established communications with his air support.[39]

The air support question, also noted in the USMC official history, begs the question of what kind of air-ground team was functioning in the brigade. As noted earlier, the two carriers had entered Sasebo on 28 August and 1 September, respectively, for upkeep prior to the Inchon operation. The two day fighter squadrons redeployed to Ashiya Air Base the morning of 2 September in order to support the second Naktong engagement. The ground support of the squadrons followed in marine corps and air force transports. VMF-323 launched two strike flights at 1615 and 1630 that day, but these close air support missions obviously responded to army and air force direction, not those of the brigade. It seems doubtful that, at this point, General Craig and his brigade staff had any more control over his aviation units than those of the Far East Air Force, although he likely counted upon their taking any measure necessary to catch up with the ground war.[40]

In fact, the close air support section of the air control squadron had detached from the brigade's command post on 20 August, returning to the South Korean naval base at Chinhae, where the air control squadron and observation squadron had maintained their permanent camp since 3 August. There, the men had performed equipment maintenance and resupply, and had no doubt caught some rest and relaxation before the planned embarkation at Pusan for the Inchon landing. The air control squadron's after-action report indicates that the close air support section marched to the sound of the guns and acted independently.[41]

On 1 September, close air support section personnel mounted their vehicles on oral orders to support the 2nd Division and the marine brigade. Traveling the distance in only four hours, they reached the command post of the army division and remained there the next day planning with the brigade's staff for the attack.

On 3 September, thirty-six Corsairs came on station during the day and were assigned four missions under marine forward air controllers, and three self-directed search-and-attack missions. The next day, forty aircraft checked in and were handed over to forward controllers for nine missions for the brigade, one more to the army, and six for search-and-attack missions. Apparently nobody needed to advise marine aviation that the fight was on.

The final tactical scheme worked out with 2nd Division on 2 September entailed movement forward by the 5th Marines early the next morning into the lines of the 9th Infantry on either side of the Yongsan Road, on high ground some eight hundred yards west of the town. The planned 0800 attack of the 5th Marines for the first time used two battalions on line: 1st Battalion on the left and 2nd Battalion to the right of the main supply route.[42]

The Second Naktong battle for the marine brigade progressed much more smoothly than its predecessor, perhaps for several reasons. The preparations, although somewhat hurried, did not produce the same confusion as before, and many lessons had been learned about the proper employment of supporting arms and combat support, such as tanks. The 5th Marines arrived, assembled, and fought the battle over all-too familiar terrain. Finally, it must be recognized that the North Korean 9th Division scarcely had the same strength or mettle as the 4th Division had displayed. The former had been reorganized in Seoul after beginning its wartime service as the 3rd Constabulary Brigade. It fought understrength with many raw recruits, having left one regiment behind at Inchon. At the Second Naktong, the 9th Division thus engaged in its first major operation of the war.[43]

Although the opening actions on 3 September provided a few of the by-now typical surprises for the marines, they only experienced only a few truly tough situations. Moving forward in the early morning from their assembly areas east of Yongsan, they encountered both army and enemy troops near and in the village, instead of farther west, where the 9th Infantry had set in its position the previous night. The North Koreans had hit those positions, held tenuously by two American infantry and one combat engineer company, and a fluid situation now

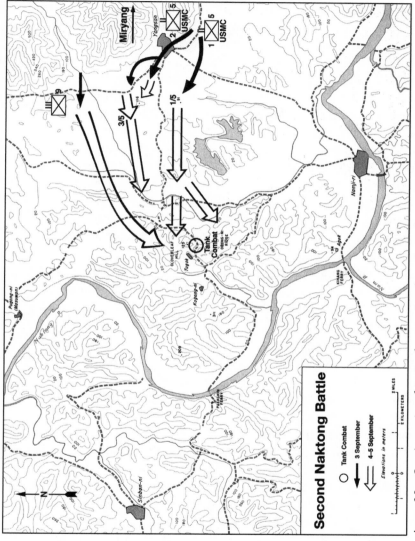

Army Map Service, printed in Appleman, *South to the Naktong, North to the Yalu: June–November, 1950.* Modified by W. Stephen Hill.

greeted the marines of the 1st Battalion and 2nd Battalions as they came up the road and veered south and north of the main supply route upon reaching the village.[44]

The 9th Infantry Regiment had fought throughout the previous day to repel the enemy attack on Yongsan, destroying several T-34 tanks in the process with 3.5-inch rocket launchers and their accompanying medium tank support. As its leading riflemen advanced, Lieutenant Colonel Roise's battalion engaged snipers and infiltrators in the village and continued across intermediate high ground toward the lines of the 9th infantry, accompanied by the tanks of First Lieutenant Robert Winter's 2nd Platoon. The marines came upon a startling sight presented by army tanks and troops fighting from the lower elevations against North Korean troops occupying the higher ridges fronting the Hill 116 mass. Those ridges, held the day before by the 9th Infantry, collectively comprised the intended jumping-off point for Roise's men. Now the 2nd Battalion, 5th Marines and its tanks engaged in a lively firefight to drive the enemy back. So exposed was the enemy to the surprise appearance of the marines, that a literal shooting gallery ensued. The tanks drew up on line near the army vehicles and the tank commanders forgot their instructions to stay down in their turrets, instead manning their topside .50-caliber machine guns to augment the fire of their turreted cannon and machine guns. North Korean fire hit several of the tanks and Lieutenant Winter fell off his M26, shot through the throat just as General Craig arrived to watch the fight. Craig rushed to assist the stricken officer and was shocked to identify Winter, his own godson. Winter, with aplomb, pointed to his tank and urged Craig to take a bottle of whiskey that he had inside, knowing that he'd not need it for a while.[45]

Notwithstanding the confusion encountered at Hill 116, the marines won the firefight in less than an hour. Without pausing, D and E Companies, supported by fire from the static tanks, surged forward on the right flank through and around the village of Myong. On the south side of the main supply route, Newton's 1st Battalion attacked at 0855, from a position still too far to the south of the road. His leading squads veered northwest into low ridges and surrounding rice paddies. Supported by ample artillery, mortar, and tank fire, as well as strikes by marine fighter-bombers, Newton's marines had a relatively easy time clearing the hill designated as their first objective.

Desperate to escape the 1st Battalion's onslaught, the North Koreans fled across the road right into the 2nd Battalion's zone of advance.[46]

The tanks of the 2nd Platoon advanced forward and parallel to the road, engaging light antitank guns and machine guns after cresting a ridge. The replacement tank platoon leader was killed by machine-gun fire, but the tanks shot up the offending gun positions and then destroyed three T-34s caught advancing up the road from the valley between the Tugok and Obong ridge systems. The 3rd Tank Platoon also advanced in support of the 1st Battalion, destroying two more T-34s along the way.[47]

Also engaging these enemy weapons was the 75mm recoilless rifle platoon of the 5th Marines antitank company, operating in support of the 2nd Platoon tanks, then under fire. Sergeant Lewis W. Zwarka ran forward when some of the gun crews became casualties, ignoring enemy fire as he made several trips to assist in carrying out the wounded. He then joined another gun crew and assisted it in redeploying the gun closer to the road, when he was cut down and killed by enemy fire.[48]

The southern arm of the 5th Marines attack swept over the high ground and the main supply route, firing at the fleeing enemy crossing the valley to the west with their own weapons and calling supporting arms down on the hapless foe. The riflemen of the 1st Battalion began occupying their final objective of the day at 1630. In the distance stood Obong Ridge, their nemesis of the previous month. To the north, the 2nd Battalion encountered more resistance, and D Company took serious casualties as it tried to secure a foothold attacking from the northeast into the Hill 116 mass.

Private First Class Frank B. Billings, a volunteer replacement rifleman from the brigade's service detachment, went into action for the first time with two other marines in a D company fire team. Climbing the steep hill, the three men advanced far ahead of the rest of the company, actually passing into the enemy lines. They immediately began to fire on North Korean machine-gun nests, knocking out two of the automatic weapons and killing several enemy soldiers before Billings himself was killed by the third machine gun. By 1900, the battalion could advance no further, having sustained 18 killed and 77 wounded, mostly in D Company. The attackers consolidated their defensive positions for the night, sending a platoon to cover the gap on the battalion's right, where the 9th Infantry had advanced, keeping abreast of the marines.[49]

No North Korean counterattack developed during the night, a signal that the enemy offensive had already reached its limit. Torrential rains began to fall, the by-product of a typhoon that had crossed Japan. The rain and surprisingly cold night temperatures would add a new dose of misery in the field. Overnight, the riflemen of the 3rd Battalion, 5th Marines prepared to pass through 2nd Battalion and continue the attack across Hill 116. The enemy had already accepted his defeat of the previous day, however, and made little effort to oppose the advance, continuing to fall back to Obong Ridge and the Cloverleaf Hill-Tugok positions.

The following day (4 September) brought terror for those North Korean soldiers still remaining between the 5th Marines lines and those distant hills. Moving rapidly against light resistance, the 3rd Battalion had overrun the entire mass of Hill 116 by 1530 while the 1st Battalion advanced another one thousand yards to the forward slopes of Observation Hill, reaching its destination by 1505 without meeting any resistance. Marines and army troops found large numbers of enemy dead and wrecked or abandoned equipment, testifying to the deadly artillery and air bombardments of the previous days.[50]

The frontage of the 5th Marines narrowed at this point because the 9th Infantry's slower advance on the right and the movement of the 1st Battalion, 5th Marines on the left effectively "pinched out" the 3rd Battalion, 5th Marines from advancing beyond the western slopes of Hill 116. That night, the enemy again made no moves against the 5th Marines, but did attack, through the rain, into a company of the 9th Infantry just to the north of the 3rd Battalion's positions. At day-break on 5 September, the machine gunners of Taplett's two rifle companies and his headquarters harried the enemy troops with long-range fire, dealing them a final blow as the army troops repelled the assault.[51]

The typhoon-induced weather front continued to shower rain on the battlefield, resulting in decreased visibility that limited the use of air support. The attack plan for 5 September proved modest enough, calling for the 1st Battalion, 5th Marines and the adjacent 9th Infantry to the north to simply advance through the abandoned enemy positions on the western slopes and on to the valley floor in front of Obong Ridge and Cloverleaf Hill, respectively. At midday, Lieutenant Colonel Murray ordered the 3rd Battalion, 5th Marines to cross behind and to the left of the 1st Battalion, relieving the latter's A Company and in doing so again bringing two battalions on line in the regimental zone. Artillery and mortar fire continued to drop on the 5th Marines, inflicting most of the casualties of the day. The enemy could be seen digging in and firing weapons of all calibers from the dominant terrain they still controlled. Despite the previous day's events, the North Korean 9th Division had not been routed and may have executed a more skillful withdrawal than the American units could appreciate. As the Americans came within small-arms range of the North Korean-held hills, some four hundred troops and three T-34 tanks emerged at 1420 from concealed positions in Tugok village and fell upon Captain Fenton's B Company on the right flank of the 1st Battalion.[52]

In the ensuing firefight—really a classic meeting engagement of armor and infantry—the enemy was decimated and repelled with apparent ease. However, the fight was hardly clean or elegant, just a brawl in which the more steady troops prevailed. The enemy machine guns and mortars on Obong Ridge chimed in with supporting fire as the well-prepared North Korean assault emerged. The riflemen and antitank men of 1st Battalion's B Company exposed themselves to hostile fire in order to attack the enemy infantry and tanks, while Lieutenant Colonel Newton brought his own mortars into play and sent his battalion antitank teams to the critical point.

As fate would have it, Lieutenant Pomeroy's 1st Tank Platoon edged down the main supply route with turrets trained on the Obong Ridge weapons that were then firing on Captain Fenton's company. The men in the tanks thus did not see the T-34s and remained unaware of their presence until 85mm armor piercing rounds from the enemy machines smashed into the two leading M26 tanks, stopping them and blocking the road for the tanks that followed. These vehicles immediately withdrew to seek firing positions, as did the M26s of the 3rd Tank Platoon behind them. Subsequently, however, the three T-34s were destroyed by rocket launcher fire.

Lieutenant Colonel Newton sent two platoons from A Company to assist Captain Fenton. Marine and army artillery also opened fire, along with Newton's mortars. The enemy attack lasted only thirty minutes, yet had come as close as one hundred yards to Fenton's position. In the space of one square kilometer, the remains of six T-34 and two M26 tanks now marked the site of the two Naktong battles. A relative quiet descended on the battlefield after 1500. B Company had broken the enemy assault at a cost of two killed and twenty-six wounded.[53]

The appearance of night fighters from VMF(N)-513 over the enemy positions on the night of 4–5 September earned special mention in the marine corps official history, but Lieutenant Colonel Murray, writing in his after action report, laconically summarized the event: "Night fighters were on station at night for the first time." That was the last air support the brigade would see, and the typhoon lashed the air bases in Japan with even greater force.[54]

As the tired riflemen gazed up at the machine guns that the North Korean again set up along Obong Ridge, they could not know that their salvation was at hand. General Walker had already ordered the relief of the marine brigade late on the night of 4 September, effective at midnight the next day, having exhausted his pleas to MacArthur that he retain it for the vital defense of the Pusan Perimeter. Even Walker's staff wondered how the priorities of higher headquarters stacked up when their fate still hung in the balance in the Pusan position:

> In midst of this obscure situation, orders were received from higher headquarters that the 1st Marine Brigade would be released by midnight 5 September, shipped to Pusan and readied for outloading. Orders to that effect accordingly sent on 4 September to the CG, 2nd Division and the CG, 1st Marine Brigade. At the same time, the CG, 2nd Division was informed that the 3rd BCT [battalion combat team], 23rd Infantry would be returned to him as soon as possible on 5 September, and that, therefore, no further reserves would be available to him except those available from his own resources.[55]

At 1530, units of the 9th Infantry made contact with B Company on the right flank of the 1st Battalion, 5th Marines; at 1725, Lieutenant Colonel Newton received orders to withdraw upon relief by soldiers of the 23rd Infantry. Newton's battalion pulled out last from the Naktong battlefield, some thirty minutes after midnight, thus making good on the promises of Generals MacArthur and Walker to their senior marines, Generals Shepherd and Smith, that the brigade would be withdrawn in time for use in the Inchon landings. The men of the 2nd Battalion, 5th Marines had already departed their rearward reserve positions late in the afternoon. General Craig noted in his journal the deteriorating conditions encountered by the exhausted marines: "Rain was falling and the roads and fields becoming muddy and I visualized a bad night for all. Army regiments [sic] soon began to arrive and relieved the brigade on the lines and the long trip back to Pusan began. A relief at night is a complicated matter but by daylight it had been completed and the last element of my command was entrucked and on the way back."[56]

Years later, Murray remembered how, at midnight, "we withdrew in a heavy, heavy rain, mud, miserable, but I was real proud that we were good enough that we could do this, where in World War II, I don't think anybody could ever have thought of doing something like that."[57]

While the brigade's air group flew ninety-one daylight fighter sorties at the Second Naktong, the artillery of the 1st Battalion, 11th Marines turned in its most impressive effort: 171 missions and 4,714 rounds being fired from 3 to 5 September, reportedly all in support of the 5th Marines. But in the case of aircraft, not all these supported the ground units of the brigade. For example, on 2 and 5 September, marine aircraft flew twenty-nine sorties in support of the army.[58]

From the standpoint of the marine corps, however, the Pusan Perimeter campaign ended with a principal irony. The men of the marine brigade thought that they had contributed in a major way to the defensive victory of the Eighth Army and then shifted to play an equally vital role in the upcoming Inchon amphibious assault that would break the back of the North Korean forces in the war.

In reality, the Eighth Army was never able to reverse the North Korean advances of September and restore the Pusan Perimeter on its original lines. That achievement would await the Inchon landing of 15 September on the west coast of Korea and the subsequent defeat of North Korean forces in and around Seoul. It is true that the 25th Infantry Division never lost Masan and that the army troops recovered some of ground taken by the North Koreans in the division's center; as well, the marine brigade's assembly area of early August at Chingdong remained intact to anchor the final lines there. Elsewhere, however, the situation remained grim. The northern third of the Pusan Perimeter held by the South Korean troops had mostly fallen to the enemy. The port of Pusan would not be recovered before the general U.N. offensive and breakout at the end of the month, in the aftermath of the Inchon landing. Taegu remained hemmed in on three sides, and only the 1st Cavalry Division held on to a section of the old left bank defenses on the Naktong River. The 2nd Infantry Division never advanced beyond the lines the 5th Marines had regained for them, facing Obong Ridge and the Cloverleaf. In the later breakout, the well-worn 9th Infantry was held up for days by the enemy on Hill 201, the last promontory on the east side of the Naktong River in the extreme southwest corner of the Naktong Bulge.

The Eighth Army saved itself in the final September battles against the North Koreans, but only narrowly so. The army's salvation was attributable in large measure to the stellar performance of several "fire brigades," among them the British 27th Brigade, and the 27th and 35th Infantry Regiments of the U.S. Army's 25th Infantry Division. The marine brigade would be missed sorely after 5 September and General Walker merited some sympathy in his losing fight with MacArthur to retain it within Eighth Army command.

Equally to be missed were the two marine corps two fighter squadrons involved in the perimeter campaign. Once committed to battle, marine aviators had flown almost daily in support of army and marine corps units alike, as orders dictated and opportunity afforded. Upon the departure of the marine squadrons, Lieutenant General Stratemeyer had to bring in an air force fighter wing with two more fighter squadrons from the Twentieth Air Force in Okinawa to make up the difference.

Operation Demon III landing at Camp Pendleton, California, 12 May 1950. The 1950 training program carried out in the reformed 1st Marine Division may have provided the margin of victory in Korea for the 1st Provisional Marine Brigade. (USMC)

Camp Pendleton buzzed with activity in early July 1950 as the brigade prepared for service overseas. Here, men of 1st Battalion, 11th Marines band gasoline cans for shipment. (USMC)

Marines wait their turn to board transport USS *Pickaway* at San Diego Naval Base. The landing ship to their rear remains in inactive reserve, also known as "mothballs." (USMC)

A machine-gun squad boards its assigned transport at San Diego, 12 July 1950. The canvas P1936 field leggings shown in this and the preceding photo remained a characteristic identifier of marine corps troops in the field. The ankle-height field shoes made these a necessary part of combat gear. (USMC)

Late arrivals that almost missed the departure of the brigade's shipping, the HO3S-1 helicopters for Marine Observation Squadron Six (VMO-6) provided yeoman duty to the brigade from forward landing zones and the Chinhae naval base in Korea. (USMC)

Somewhere in the Pacific Ocean: marines on board transport USS *Clymer* fire their M1918A2 Browning Automatic Rifles (BAR), some undoubtedly for the first time. (USMC)

Pusan harbor, 2 August 1950, USS *George Clymer* ties up pierside. This is the discouragingly routine sight that greeted Brig. Gen. Edward A. Craig as he anxiously awaited the debarkation of his command, alerted (he thought) to move at once toward the front. (USMC)

Gen. Craig boards USS *Clymer* at Pusan, 2 August 1950, for a terse reunion with his command. (USMC)

Marines route march off the Pusan piers to trucks and railroad cars for movement to the nearby front. (USMC)

Marines at the Pusan railroad station, on their first full day ashore. (USMC)

110

The first "colors" ceremony in Korea for the marine brigade, in bivouac;
Brig. Gen. Craig (third from right) and his staff render honors. (USMC)

Newly arrived at Changwon, the men of the marine brigade immediately encountered the heat and humidity and rough terrain of Korea as they dug in their first outpost positions. (USMC)

Moving up against North Korean forces, marine corps riflemen wear World War II–vintage uniforms and are equipped with weapons and gear from the previous conflict. (USMC)

Not all of their equipment was outdated. These M26 tanks had been acquired postwar over several years and saw their first Marine Corps action within a few days of their arrival at Pusan: Tanks of 2nd platoon, A Company parked near the brigade command post, 9 August 1950. (U.S. Army)

Another new weapon was the 75mm recoilless rifle, which had replaced the antitank guns of the previous war. This army 75mm recoilless rifle (1st Cavalry Division) covers a position on the Naktong sector north of where the marine brigade would fight, 21 August 1950. (U.S. Army)

Flight deck handlers on USS *Badoeng Strait* arm F4U-4B Corsairs of VMF-323 with 5-inch rockets, September 1950. Throughout the campaign, the two day fighter squadrons struck daily at the enemy, often in direct support of brigade units engaged in combat. (USMC)

Eighth Army commander Lt. Gen. Walton Walker (left) visits Maj. Gen. John Church (center) at the latter's command post, 24th Infantry Division, 13 August 1950, the day Walker ordered elements of two more army regiments to assist the division at the First Battle of the Naktong. (U.S. Army)

Action imminent, 16 August: marines wash off the road dust as the marine brigade's convoys arrive at the Miryang assembly area before entering the First Naktong battle. (U.S. Army)

Marine tanks and infantry advance past burning villages toward the First Naktong battle. (USMC)

105mm howitzers of 1st Battalion, 11th Marines fire in support of 5th Marines during the First Naktong, while a wary lookout watches the nearby hills for signs of infiltrators. (USMC)

Mortar crews fire their 81mm battalion mortar during the First Naktong. (USMC)

Riflemen of 1st Battalion, 5th Marines file past an A Company M26 disabled by a broken track during the First Naktong. (USMC)

South Korean bearers during the First Naktong. (USMC)

A 75mm recoilless rifle team of the Antitank Company, 5th Marines fires at North Korean positions on Obong Ridge during the First Naktong. (USMC)

5th Marines advance against North Korean resistance in the Naktong Bulge, 18–19 August. (U.S. Army)

A Company tanks fire at enemy positions across the Naktong River, 18 August. (U.S. Army)

Assault rocket teams of the Antitank Company, 5th Marines move past their first tank targets during the First Naktong. (USMC)

Marines of 3rd Battalion, 5th Marines relax on the slopes of Hill 311 as the enemy flees across the Naktong, 19 August 1950. (USMC)

A Company's dozer tank clears away wrecked T-34s after the First Naktong, 19 August 1950. (USMC)

Marines fire at retreating North Koreans at the end of the First Naktong. (USMC)

View of the Bean Patch, August 1950, where the brigade stood down in operational reserve between the Naktong battles. (USMC)

A mobile laundry unit of the Service Company provided some of the minimal luxuries in Korea. (USMC)

Army leaders confer in Korea, 23 August 1950, when it seemed that the North Korean offensives had been halted. Left to right are Maj. Gen. William B. Kean (25th Infantry Division), Lt. Gen. Walker, Gen. Collins. (U.S. Army)

Marine M26 tanks roll into position as 5th Marines approach the Naktong battlefield on 3 September 1950. (USMC)

Marines man a .30-caliber M1919A4 machine gun, 3 September 1950. (USMC)

Marine riflemen and tanks at the Second Naktong occupy positions in front of Hill 116 on 3 September; Marine M26 tanks advance up the road on the far right. This is probably the push by 1st Battalion, 5th Marines and the 3rd Tank Platoon that finished North Korean resistance during the melee of that morning. (USMC)

4

REORGANIZATION AND RECORDING

The Brigade's Legacy

The bulk of the 5th Marines and supporting troops rode trucks back to Pusan, but the heavy equipment, including the tanks, had to board trains for their return to the port, arriving around 2200 on 6 September. Many of the brigade's marines relished their last sight of the trains, which had too often halted in numerous tunnels, spewing stack gasses from their coal-fired boilers into the murky gloom and threatening the men with asphyxiation.[1]

At the port, the marines went into a new bivouac, where they found more replacements and the new third rifle companies at last sent from the United States to join the three infantry battalions. As if integrating new units and preparing the embarkation for the upcoming Inchon landings were not enough, the marine brigade also received responsibility for training some twenty-six hundred South Korean marines. Commanded by Colonel-Commandant Shin Hyun Joon, the Korean Marine Corps Regiment would fight with the 1st Marine Division as an extra fourth infantry regiment, beginning with the Inchon landings. Many of these troops received their first rifle marksmanship training at the hands of the now-veteran 5th Marines at Pusan.[2]

General Shepherd visited Pusan and the marine brigade on 11 September to meet with Craig and his officers. He observed the 3rd Battalion, 5th Marines rehearsing its landing plan for Inchon and the training of the Korean marines, and conferred with Craig's staff on the integration of replacements and the plans for Inchon. Heartened by what he saw and heard, he stated, "I believe that the Brigade is ready. Their spirit is fine—all they want is to get a foot on the beach and they say they will take their objective. It was really inspiring to talk to them."[3]

NEXT MISSION

Some ships already stood at the quay as the brigade filed into Pusan, and the arduous loading of ships of the navy's Task Force 90 began on 8 September. General Craig began daily planning and briefings with his key officers on board USS *Cavalier* on 6 August at 2000, continued on successive days from a command post set up in the campus of Pusan University. The 5th Marines, logically, received the most critical missions in the assault plan because they had already seen combat. The regiment's first assault element, comprising the 1st Battalion plus six tanks and an engineer detachment, was to seize the harbor island of Wolmi-do early on the morning on 15 September, leaving the rest of the 5th Marines to attack the port of Inchon proper at the next high tide. Craig shifted his command post to the *Cavalier* on 11 September, and the ships sailed the next day at 1430. At sea, en route to the Inchon operating area, the 1st Provisional Marine Brigade officially disbanded, and its constituent organizations reverted to the 1st Marine Division and the 1st Marine Aircraft Wing.[4]

Already at sea, the escort carriers engaged in steady daytime flight operations with their Corsair squadrons embarked. Their upkeep completed, the ships had sortied from Sasebo on 5 September. Once they had landed the fighters of VMF-214 and VMF-323, launching commenced and, despite the bad weather, VMF-323 put up a combat air patrol; but it had to land at Ashiya Air Base in the afternoon. VMF-214 managed to launch eight fighters in two flights in the afternoon, and they flew some interdiction missions near the Naktong River. But commencing the next day, the squadrons began continuous operations against the North Koreans all over the peninsula through the Inchon landings (15 September) and the rest of the month, the carriers replenishing at anchorage near Inchon from fleet auxiliary shipping.[5]

Although not part of the story of the 1st Marine Brigade, it bears mentioning that the two fighter squadrons and the 5th Marines soon made decisive contributions to the Inchon-Seoul campaign. Coming directly out of the Pusan Perimeter battles, the 5th Marines carried out the most difficult operations of the Inchon landing, seized Kimpo Airfield, and then crossed the Han River to envelop the capital city itself. But before Kimpo fell, the hard-luck 1st Platoon of A Company, 1st Tank Battalion finally took its revenge, savaging a column of six T-34 tanks and hundreds of accompanying North Korean infantrymen early on the morning of 17 September. This engagement took place when the North Koreans blundered into the lines of the 2nd Battalion, 5th Marines. Infantryman and tankers therefore shared the kills, as well as credit for the victory, but the previously chastised tankers felt with good reason that they had finally come into their own.

While the brigade struggled to load their ships at Pusan, General Shepherd sent his preliminary compliments to corps logisticians, praising them for the evident miracles they had performed in keeping marine combat units supplied and commending them for their efficiency and cooperation throughout the crisis. A copy of this message was routed through Headquarters Marine Corps (HQMC), where an anonymous staffer in the Plans and Policies Department commented, in pencil: "Everyone gets a commendation except HQMC."[6]

AFTER ACTION REPORTS AND INTERPRETING THE EVENTS

General Shepherd's congratulatory mood carried him through almost the rest of the year. Although overshadowed by the evident success of the 1st Marine Division in the Inchon-Seoul campaign and the U.N. drive into North Korea, the accomplishments of the marine brigade in the Pusan Perimeter played well into his major professional objectives during this period of his career. He and other senior officers of his generation still smarted from the difficulties of the defense reform initiatives of the late 1940s, as well as the fiscal impoverishment of the marine corps by the end of the decade. Shepherd thus ensured in his remaining years as commanding general in the Pacific and subsequently as USMC commandant that the Korean War record would deliver the maximum benefits to the marine corps as an institution in the U.S. military establishment.

It should therefore surprise no one that the story of that success had already taken form in a matter of weeks. Shepherd's liaison cell embedded in MacArthur's naval component command labored quickly to produce an initial record of the events for Washington's consumption that set the tone and substance for the preferred marine corps version for all time.[7]

The staff review constructed a dramatic narrative of the situation existing on 2 August 1950. According to this account, the 1st Provisional Marine Brigade arrived on the scene when the morale of United Nations forces stood at its lowest and Communist aggressors flushed with recent victories were advancing steadily toward Pusan and the sea. Debarked at Pusan and quickly dispatched to the front, the brigade immediately engaged in combat at a time when *all adjacent ground units stood on the defensive and most were withdrawing.* The *numerically superior* enemy in the brigade sector had *been advancing against negligible opposition and was well on its way toward the seizure of the Masan-Chinhae complex and a final plunge toward Pusan.* But here the enemy collided hard in a moving engagement with U.N. forces, which (one infers for the first time) did not give way and pressed the battle with more conviction and effect. The results were conclusive. In four days the marine brigade, utilizing its devastating carrier-based organic close air support in a manner *not previously experienced by U.N. forces,* advanced twenty-six miles against a shattered and torn enemy, now retreating for the first time. The marine brigade was later withdrawn before its advance had been halted in order to realign the U.N. front. Its opposition, the enemy 6th Division, *although later reconstituted, never again was employed as an effective fighting force.*

Withdrawn to reserve soon thereafter, the marine brigade engaged in another "shocking action" almost immediately against an enemy unit that had crossed the Naktong River in force and was penetrating U.N. lines. In a series of bitter battles, the enemy was stopped then later thrown back after considerable losses in personnel and equipment. The brigade then reverted to reserve and moved to Pusan for embarkation preparatory to the Inchon-Seoul operations. Another enemy crossing of the Naktong again endangered the U.N. defensive perimeter. The brigade, urgently recalled from Pusan, moved to the front and engaged the spearheading enemy 9th Division, with the same results as before: *after having to fight its way to the line of departure, the brigade, again using its organic carrier-based aircraft in the most daring type of close air support, launched a counterattack which carried over six miles in three days and resulted in an enemy withdrawal back across the Naktong.*

Recommitment of the brigade to the defense of the Eighth Army perimeter had delayed scheduled embarkation, movement, and re-equipment to such an extent *that plans had to be altered and the brigade was rushed from Pusan for the Inchon operation.* Briefing and most of the re-equipping for the Inchon operation was accomplished later on board ship.

This sensational tale, closely paraphrased above from the original text, might easily be mistaken as a press release by a casual reader. But it was not a press release, and its readership was by no means casual. Sent to the chief of naval operations and the Pacific Fleet commander as an encoded message with a "secret" classification, it was accordingly routed throughout the naval establishment. That its contents met the approval of Shepherd seems most likely given his own diary entry of 22 August, written at the halfway point of the campaign, while visiting the brigade at Masan:

> The Brigade has done a splendid job and pulled the chestnuts out of the fire for the Army on several occasions. Neither Stewart nor Craig spoke any words of criticism about the Army staff work or activities of Army units with which they have been fighting, but it was apparent from the movements of the Brigade and the orders and counter orders they had received, that the staff planning by the Eighth Army and the 25th Division was of a low order and that the Army troops with whom they had been fighting were very mediocre. . . .
>
> It was also apparent from the scheme of maneuver for the Battle of the Naktong River Bulge, that the Brigade had carried the bulk of the load in being ordered to attack three principal well defended hill masses, while the other two regiments of the task force were only assigned to assault one hill.
>
> To demonstrate the amount of jumping around that they had done, it was calculated that one battalion had covered 325 miles in the two weeks they had been engaged.[8]

These incredibly myopic viewpoints of the actions of the marine brigade at Pusan almost immediately became established marine corps lore that would endure to the present day with scarcely any critical examination: the marine brigade arrived in Pusan amidst chaos and defeat and, thanks to its superior fighting ability and organic aircraft, repeatedly and consistently outperformed the lackluster and substandard army units and in doing so almost singlehandedly turned what was shaping up to be a crushing defeat into a decisive victory over the North Korean invaders.

Shepherd continued his quest to establish the best possible position for the corps, using this cooked, skewed, and biased record of the Korean War. As commandant of the marine corps (1952–1956), he ordered a study by the Marine Corps Board to determine in tactical terms the "influence of Marine Corps forces upon the course of the Korean War." It therefore comes as no surprise that during his tenure as commandant, the marine corps published the first official histories of the Korean War produced by any of the U.S. armed forces. A writing team led by civilian author Lynn Montross, a veteran freelancer who began working for the marine corps in 1950, produced two of the five volumes bearing Shepherd's own signature, precisely covering the Pusan Perimeter and Inchon campaigns. The remainder of the series took many more years to complete, the last volume in 1972.

The staff study, to its credit, did provide some corrective interpretations to the sensational and false rhetoric of the October 1950 message. It recognized the Eighth Army's use of the 27th Infantry as a reserve striking force (or "fire brigade") analogous to the marine brigade, and that serious combat actions occurred within the army's area of operations in which the marine brigade took no part. However, the tactical analyses it provided did not reflect careful study of the circumstances surrounding the employment of the brigade.

For instance, concerning the brigade's Sachon operation, the board characterized Sachon as the final objective of Task Force Kean and asserted that the brigade and its aircraft had been "thus employed against the most dangerous Communist threat then existent."[9] The designation of Chinju as the Eighth Army objective of the operation and the deployment of both the 34th Infantry and RCT 5 against it somehow escaped the notice of the board. The board's report identified the enemy in the brigade zone of action as consisting of at least two North Korean infantry regiments, supported by artillery and probably tanks. The study depicted attacks by the 2nd and 3rd Battalions of the 5th Marines at Chingdong as smoothly executed seizures of high ground held by elements of these regiments, using air support. The report further credited Lieutenant Cahill's platoon as *taking an enemy-held hill* on 7 August and holding it against counterattacks by strong forces until relieved by the 2nd Battalion, 5th Marines a mere twenty-four hours later.

At this point, the report credited the 2nd and 3rd Battalions with killing an estimated one thousand enemy soldiers. The board saw the battle for Kosong as a fight against enemy delaying actions on the outskirts and in the town itself. The actions by the 3rd Battalion, 5th Marines in clearing Bloody Gulch and searching for survivors of the overrun RCT 5 artillery batteries somehow (in the board version of the events) resulted in some three hundred enemy casualties; and since RCT 5 was cut off from supply and had not approached its objective of Chinju, the Eighth Army cancelled further operations of Task Force Kean, leaving the brigade a mere two miles from Sachon, its right flank exposed by the failure of RCT 5 to advance. According to the board, the enemy's early morning attack of 13 August fell on the brigade, not just B Company, and was beaten off at a cost of three hundred enemy dead, thanks to artillery and mortar fire, followed by fighter-bomber strikes after daybreak. Despite some confusion in its presentation, the report claims with certainty at least nineteen hundred enemy killed by the operations of the brigade while part of Task Force Kean.

Totally ignoring the army's efforts and achievements in several days of fighting against the North Korean 6th Division west of Masan, the board found that the brigade had routed the North Korean 83rd Motorized Regiment, "considered to be among the best trained in the NK Army and principally employed in offensive action." The marine brigade "constituted a *spearhead* [author's italics] in this the first instance of a truly major offensive action by U.N. forces since the inception of hostilities in Korea; contributed a major proportion of the effort required to defeat the enemy penetration; blunted and broke the enemy's critical thrust at the southern flank; [and] wiped out the enemy threat in his area."[10]

The board's report improved in its description of the two Naktong battles and in each case acknowledged the employment of the army's 27th Infantry as another "fire brigade" on other sectors of the Pusan front. Once again, however, the actions of army units involved in the same operation are distorted.[11] For example, according to the report, "The Naktong Bulge contained three large hill masses and commanded the general area in that part of the Eighth Army lines. The enemy had occupied these areas and it was for the purpose of clearing these three hill masses that the Brigade was committed in this sector." While in the main a fair statement, it does not indicate that the 24th Infantry Division had already been given the 9th Infantry as an early "fire brigade" reinforcement, and that army forces had worn down the attacking 4th North Korean Division considerably, pushing it back to the hills, but lacked the offensive power to eradicate the Naktong bridgehead. The reduction of the three hill masses, as noted in the previous chapter, fell to the marine brigade operating in the *southern half* of the Naktong Bulge; however, the northern half of the enemy bridgehead was retaken by the counterattacks of the 9th Infantry to seize Turok village and Cloverleaf Hill in the center, while the weaker 19th and 34th Infantry Regiments captured three ridges dominating the Naktong River left bank, upstream from the marine brigade's zone of action.

The Marine Corps Board report faulted the 9th Infantry for *failing to attack* on the right flank of the 5th Marines, and stated inaccurately that when Newton's 1st Battalion attacked through Roise's 2nd Battalion "with the aid of constant close tactical air support and heavy ground supporting fires *most of the ridge* was seized by nightfall."[author's italics][12]

In the ensuing actions, the board's report credited the marine brigade with destroying all four of the T-34s attacking it on 17 August, and again faulted the 9th Infantry for failing to support the marine advance (by the 3rd Battalion, assaulting Hill 311), neglecting to mention that the 9th Infantry had been pinched out of any further advance the day before, *as planned*. The report further asserted that marine aircraft provided the "bulk of heavy supporting fires" and that the enemy had carried his attacks out at night primarily to avoid the brigade's aircraft. As for the tank attack, marines handily defeated it, and "decisively proved that T-34 Russian tanks were not impervious to American weapons and that well planned and vigorously executed attacks against them had every chance of success." Actually, the 9th Infantry had destroyed several of these tanks earlier in the Naktong Bulge fight, and American and ROK troops had been destroying them with all available weapons for weeks. In conclusion, the report asserts that the marines fought all three regiments of the 4th North Korean Division.

The report deftly concluded that, "If the brigade had not been present to halt 4th NK Division after the 27th Infantry had been sent north [to the Taegu sector], lines would have been cut, the bulk of U.N. forces severed from their base of supply, and Pusan a possible prey to NK aggression." The board went on to claim an estimated forty-five hundred casualties inflicted on the 4th Division.[13]

The recommitment of the brigade to the Pusan campaign in the Naktong sector somehow attracted the board's attention as seriously interrupting the brigade's preparations for the Inchon operation two weeks later. As noted previously, General Craig and his staff had received only sketchy information from the 1st Marine Division about the pending operation. However, the board's report relates that the brigade "was belatedly engaged in amphibious planning and on 1 Sep all units were engaged in moving heavy equipment and supplies to the Pusan area for embarkation. On this date CG, Eighth Army, with 27th Infantry already heavily engaged, ordered 1st Prov MarBrig, the other 'fire brigade,' to prepare for possible action. All activities with respect to embarkation were halted." One searches in vain through the records of the brigade and its units for evidence of this interruption. Perhaps this interpretation reflected personal testimony or interviews, but in any case it never reappeared in subsequent versions, such as the marine corps' official history.[14]

In the board's version of the Second Naktong battle, one reads of the movement of the brigade to Miryang, its opening attack through the deteriorated 9th Infantry lines, and the systematic pushing back of the 9th North Korean Division several miles over what is erroneously termed the "same terrain which Marines had fought over and seized from the enemy during the period 17–19 Aug." In this phase of operations, according to the report, the enemy suffered heavy casualties (with thirty-five hundred credited to the brigade) and loss of equipment, including four T-34 tanks and a probable fifth. No mention is made of the two M26s lost to the T-34s, and the weather restrictions hampering tactical aircraft operations of 5 August are obscured with the highly ambitious statement, "Marine all-weather aircraft were in support during the night of 4–5 Sep and coupled with the fighter squadrons provided around-the-clock tactical air support."[15]

Classified "confidential" and distributed to all operational and training commands by the commandant, this staff study revealed a penchant for self-promotion typical of all the armed forces during and after the defense reorganization reform period. The haphazard, limited, and flawed analysis notwithstanding, Lynn Montross justified

its interpretations and conclusions in the preface to his first volume
of the official marine corps history of the Korean War, which dealt
with the Pusan Perimeter.[16]

Montross and his principal co-author, Captain Nicholas A.
Canzona (who had served in the brigade's engineer company), tem-
pered the tone and stridency of the staff study to some extent in the
five-volume official history, but significantly reconciled the problem
of related operations by higher and adjacent army organizations by
ignoring much of this relevant background. What amounts to a
veiled warning is inserted in the preface of each of the five volumes;
for example, readers of the first volume, *The Pusan Perimeter*, are
greeted at the start with the following admonition: "Since this is
primarily a Marine Corps story, the activities of other services during
this period are not described in detail except to present a proper
background to the overall account."[17]

As the first major narrative of the Korean War intended for public
consumption, *The Pusan Perimeter* constituted the leading edge of
the public effort by the marine corps to fortify its niche in the national
defense establishment after the war. There seems little doubt that
the concepts stressed as a priority then and for decades thereafter
have remained fixed, these being readiness, combat effectiveness,
and the air-ground team, the last represented by so-called organic
marine corps aviation.

The language adopted by Montross and Canzona for their conclusions to the first volume reflected the analysis of the 1952 staff
study. Offsetting the brigade's losses (155 killed, 15 died of wounds,
2 missing, and 730 wounded) the board claimed that the marines had
inflicted ninety-nine hundred casualties on opposing North Korean
units. This seems a gross overestimate of both the casualties inflicted
as well as the strength of the opposing forces, detailed in the preceding
chapters. After the mid-August Naktong battle—the only engagement by the brigade that saw the marines holding the ground they
had taken in the fighting—the army reported finding twelve hundred
enemy dead. Nonetheless, Montross concluded that the "turning point
in the U.N. fortunes of war owed in no small measure to the three
counterattacks by the Marines in the Pusan Perimeter."[18]

Montross further embellished his account with praise for what
he deemed the exceptional accomplishments of the marine brigade,
lauding it as the first unit sent from the continental United States to

enter combat, even though it had been activated only six days before embarkation. He also noted how the marines, who were trained as amphibious troops, had performed superbly as infantry in the peculiar mountain terrain of Korea, thus exhibiting marine corps versatility.

But Montross was wrong on the first point: although the brigade was the first of the reinforcing units to leave the United States, it was not the first of those units to arrive or see combat in Korea. Nor were the marines unique in having to adapt to fighting in mountainous terrain: the army units that deployed to Korea were faced with the same challenge, and also adapted accordingly.

The three squadrons of tactical aircraft of MAG-33 provided the "best close air support in the history of the Marine Corps." Although the marine corps established close air support as a distinctly postwar doctrinal refinement, Montross's statistical scoreboard, "MAG-33 operations in Korea from 3 August to 14 September 1950," aimed at further embellishing the story:[19]

CLOSE AIR SUPPORT (CAS) SORTIES

Squadron	USMC	Army	ROK	CAS total	Misc. sorties	All sorties
VMF 214	337	111	60	508	162	670
VMF 323	304	83	21	408	90	498
VMF(N) 513	21	50	8	79	264	343
Totals	662	244	89	995	516	1511

These figures, also drawn from the 1952 staff study, cannot be reconciled with squadron records. The *total* tactical sorties flown on days the *brigade was engaged in combat* come to 391 for the two day fighter squadrons: 225 for 8–13 August, 104 for 17–18 August (on 19 August, squadrons flew strikes against the Naktong crossings, not close air support for the brigade), and 62 for 3–4 September. Even these squadron totals include numerous sorties striking distant targets and army targets for lack of calls from the brigade, and therefore do not qualify as close air support sorties for the marine corps units. Given the almost daily operations of the two day fighter squadrons from 3 August to 5 September, one would see little logic if the totals had in fact shown close air support mostly for the brigade's ground units. The ground units had only seen twelve days of combat operations, excluding artillery missions. The inclusion of the night fighter squadron sorties under close air support also seems very disingenuous, for no reliable air control method yet existed for night attacks close to ground troops. Night fighter sorties must therefore be classified as interdiction or more distant "direct air support" missions, in no sense under control of the brigade's forward air controllers. The inclusion of operations from 5 to 14 September remains puzzling, since the only troops then in contact with the enemy belonged to the army and allied U.N. forces. One wonders if the sorties flown before the Inchon operation against targets in the 1st Marine Division's future area of operations are counted as "close air support" in this most blatant example of cooking the books.[20]

Assessing the Campaign of 1st Provisional Marine Brigade

On the positive side, the official accounts of the brigade's deployment and operations in the Pusan Perimeter engendered much inspirational writing about the workings—and manifest virtues—of marine corps culture. In the decades following the Korean War, every marine recruit and fledgling officer learned that the brigade had fought well after deploying with virtually no notice to a previously unknown land. Marines serving in the Fleet Marine Force could reinforce their efforts day to day in training and other aspects of garrison readiness with the knowledge that, as was the case for the marine brigade in Korea, the "balloon might go up" at any moment and a marine would in short order find himself on board navy ships heading for an unfamiliar locale to fight an unknown enemy.

It remains regrettable that rhetorical excesses and exaggerations have distorted the history of the marine brigade at Pusan. It seems clear that they were propagated by the marine corps leadership in the aftermath of the campaign, largely for the advantage of the marine corps position in defense policymaking, thus reflecting the very motives that other antagonistic leaders such as Lieutenant General Stratemeyer sensed during his "three wars" of Korea: fighting the North Koreans, the other U.S. armed services, and the press. Surely, the brigade's accomplishments in Korea are in no way diminished by an accurate account of its operations, even though such an account would give full to the efforts of army and air force units in stopping or turning back North Korean attacks before General Craig and his men arrived.

The published record of the brigade in Korea has also served marine corps policymakers down to the present day. It has figured prominently in reinforcing the cherished notion of inseparable marine corps ground and aviation combat units operating under the command and operational direction of marine corps officers. This dogma took concrete form in the 1960s with the formulation of the Marine Air-Ground Task Force (MAGTF), consisting of three sizes of standing air-ground formations built around a ground combat battalion, regiment, or division in tandem with an aircraft squadron, group, or wing, each supported by a central service support echelon. The marine corps fiercely defended this doctrine against all types of interservice opposition through decades of war planning and military operations. Not coincidentally, the later volumes of the official history of the Korean War often emphasized the valiant struggle of the 1st Marine Division to have the use of its aviation support in the remaining years of the conflict; similarly, marine corps resistance to the consolidation of airspace control under air force auspices during the Vietnam War figures prominently in the ten volumes written about that conflict.

A recent study produced by the United States Marine Corps Command and Staff College promoted the brigade as an embryonic marine air-ground task force in every sense, serving to "prove" the efficacy of the task force concept well before it existed: "The Marines of the 1st Provisional Marine Brigade had accomplished something that Marines have not had to do since August of 1950. Without warning, they organized as a Marine Air Ground Task Force (MAGTF), deployed to a major theater war, and immediately entered combat against a determined and well-armed foe."[21]

Unfortunately, such *post hoc ergo propter hoc* reasoning tends to gloss over the apparent evidence that the brigade was called into being first as a ground combat regimental combat team, "one regimental combat team from FMFPac with appropriate marine air unit for tactical air support" in Admiral Sherman's words. General Shepherd then amended the orders to promote the formation of an air-ground unit in which "Marine aircraft and helicopter squadrons formed an integral part of a Marine Air-Ground Team." Actually neither Sherman nor Shepherd realized their goals, for the "brigade" operated as a ground unit commanded by General Craig under the Eighth Army, whereas the aviation component, MAG-33, operated ashore in Japan under command of the nominal deputy brigade commander, General

Cushman, who considered himself the Commanding General, 1st Marine Aircraft Wing (Forward). But even then, the group commander of MAG-33 exercised little command for the day fighter squadrons operating under the direction of Admiral Ruble, commanding Carrier Division 15, furnishing support to all ground units, but with priority given to the brigade when the latter was engaged in combat. The night fighters operated under Fifth Air Force command, leaving only the small observation squadron (VMO-6) ashore in Korea supporting General Craig. Even the two photo reconnaissance Corsairs operated by MAG-33 flew at the direction of General MacArthur's headquarters. As beneficial as F4U fighter support proved for the brigade, it was not an example of an air-ground team in operation, except in the already creative imagination of marine corps leaders.

CONCLUSION

The 1st Provisional Marine Brigade was formed in the United States as the first marine corps contribution to Korean conflict. Marines for years had maintained an excellent training routine in garrison, despite the budget limitations experienced by all U.S. forces to a varying degree. Because the marine corps was then an all-volunteer force, it was able to combine personnel from its variously under-strength units at Camp Pendleton and El Toro Air Station to fill out reduced battalions of infantry and artillery, backed by combat support and service units and a capable aircraft group, all in fairly rapid order. In other words, a mad scramble ensued to assemble from the limited personnel available a complete combat unit, capable of deploying and conducting a full range of combat missions for an unforeseeable period of time.

Of the three major reinforcing formations initially dispatched from the United States (the 1st Marine Brigade, Regimental Combat Team 5, and the 9th Infantry Regiment), the brigade departed first but arrived last, owing to the slower speed of its ships. Upon arrival in the combat theater of operations, it formed what was essentially a "cooperative" of two separate ground and aviation units, each having little combat experience (except for the veteran fighter pilots). The marine brigade was not filled out to war strength because senior commanders had decided that it would likely serve as an advance element of the complete 1st Marine Division, and would await the arrival of the division in Japan before entering combat. This ran counter to the wishes and reinforced the fears of the brigade commander. During the two-week crossing of the Pacific, much schooling and impromptu organizing necessarily ensued on board the ships.

Dispatched to Pusan instead of a training base in Japan because of Eighth Army's deteriorating situation, the brigade nevertheless arrived at a time that General Walker sensed was opportune for launching a counterattack. Accordingly, the brigade took part in the counteroffensive stroke of Task Force Kean (25th Infantry Division) against the newly arrived North Korean forces on the southern front of the Pusan Perimeter. Already battered by defensive battles fought to the west of Masan, the North Korean forces, but chiefly the 6th Division, clung doggedly to their interior positions in the Sobuk heights while delaying the advance of numerically superior U.S. forces, including the brigade's own 5th Marines, on the road to Sachon. Despite the errors common to any unit when introduced to combat for the first time, the 5th Marines surged forward and seized the enemy positions. In doing so, the marines received the same air support provided in the recent California exercise, with fighter-bombers operating from the same escort carrier class used in stateside exercises. After five days of advancing toward Sachon, Task Force Kean cancelled further offensive moves and the brigade withdrew to army reserve, subsequently to be given a new mission.

Called upon to reinforce the battered 24th Infantry Division in the Naktong Bulge, the brigade entered the zone as the third "fire brigade" deployed to that sector. Attacking in concert with the 9th Infantry and two regiments of the 24th Division, the brigade overcame tough initial resistance and then joined in the pursuit of the now shattered 4th North Korean Division to the near shore of the Naktong River.

Back in army reserve and preparing for reversion to its parent division and aircraft wing for operations on the west coast of Korea, the brigade was called upon one last time to reinforce a threatened breakthrough area, this time in the 2nd Infantry Division sector in the by-then familiar Naktong Bulge. Replenished with replacements, the brigade fought as before at over 90 percent authorized strength, albeit on a reduced establishment still lacking third rifle companies and third artillery battery gun platoons. However, the army infantry regiments were similarly hamstrung, fighting with only two infantry battalions each; what's more, the army units had been in action more less continuously for over 50 days. By now seasoned in close combat and the employment of supporting arms, the 5th Marines and its ground and air support easily handled the inexperienced North Korean 9th Division and, again with the army's 9th Infantry on its right flank, drove the enemy from his positions. At this point, the brigade had to depart the battlefield and begin its embarkation process at Pusan in order to join the Inchon invasion force at sea. That the enemy remained within the Naktong Bulge until late September provides sufficient testimony to the difference made by the marine brigade in the battles of the Pusan Perimeter.

The legacy of the marine brigade at Pusan remains clear. Undefeated in any fight, it displayed its unique marine corps hallmark constituted in peacetime readiness exercises, the fortitude produced by marine corps training and discipline, and the solidarity gained from corps traditions and culture. It perforce outperformed most other units, friendly and enemy, in the Pusan Perimeter, as one would have expected of an all-volunteer force freshly arrived on the battlefield. Carefully employed by General Walker, and capably handled by Brigadier General Craig and Lieutenant Colonel Murray, it never remained in the front lines for prolonged periods, and it pulled as much time in reserve as in combat and benefited from shorter pulses of combat action than did the larger army divisions. Although hindered by shortages of rifle companies, it was without question the most powerful organization for its size in the Eighth Army.

For the individual marines there could be no thought of failure or letting down one's brother marines—an attitude that inspired legendary feats of exertion and courage. Although no Medals of Honor were awarded to marines in the brigade, two Navy Crosses and four-teen Army Distinguished Service Crosses were awarded, along with hundreds of lesser decorations. While it is true that the Eighth Army fought its battle and saved itself in the six weeks of the Pusan Peri-meter campaign, the magnitude of its suffering would have proven much greater without the timely arrival of the 1st Provisional Marine Brigade.

As the assault transports departed Pusan and the escort carriers began launching marine corps Corsairs against new target sets in the Inchon area, the men of the brigade took away with them an intense sense of accomplishment. However, interservice rivalries had decades more to run their twisted paths. Even after the Inchon-Seoul Campaign added new laurels to the corps' record and the planning for a peace-time American presence in the Far East advanced, Douglas MacArthur provided a curiously rash and harsh judgment. In conversation with General Stratemeyer, he observed that "the Marine was an excellent amphibious landing soldier, but when it came to remaining in battle, under all hazards with mud and weather, that the man on the ground must take, the Marine did not compare with the American soldier. The Marine is a specialist; he is willing to take great losses to do a quick job, but then his desires are to pull out, accept the plaudits of the American people, and let the doughboys carry on."[22]

Within the month, MacArthur—and others—would have to recant, because yet another marine corps epic took form in the demanding battles west of the Chosin Reservoir, on the mountainous east coast of Korea.

Other illusions died hard as well, and General Craig likely never forgave Shepherd and others for failing to bring his brigade to war strength before deploying it to the Far East. Later in Washington, D.C., he again ran into what he considered another distasteful example of bureaucracy. Reporting for duty at marine headquarters as director of the marine corps reserve in his new grade of major general, Craig attended conferences that convinced him that "the Korean War was not an important subject in Washington." Appalled that the aim in Korean was now to achieve a stalemate instead of a decisive victory, and embittered that MacArthur had been summarily relieved of his command by the president, he abruptly resigned after attending a parti-cularly irksome general's conference.[23]

Perhaps in leaving the corps when he did, Craig spared himself the ignominious exploitation of his brigade's true record in the interests of interservice bickering.

APPENDIX A

Organization of the 1st Provincial Marine Brigade, 7 July–13 September 1950

Source: Montross, Lynn and Nicholas A. Canzona. *U.S. Marine Operations in Korea. Vol. 1, The Pusan Perimeter.* Washington: Historical Branch, G-3, Marine Corps, 1954.

Commanding General: Brig. Gen. Edward A. Craig
Deputy Commander: Brig. Gen. Thomas J. Cushman
Chief of Staff: Col. Edward W. Snedeker
G-1: Maj. Donald W. Sherman
G-2: Lt. Col. Ellsworth G. Van Orman
G-3: Lt. Col. Joseph L. Stewart
G-4: Lt. Col. Arthur A. Chidester

SPECIAL STAFF SECTION

Adjutant: Capt. Harold G. Schrier
Supply Officer: Maj. James K. Eagan
Air Officer: Maj. James N. Cupp
Signal Officer: Maj. Elwin M. Stimpson
Air Observer: Capt. Edwin L. Rives
Signal Supply Officer: 1st Lt. Joseph E. Conners
Engineer Supply Officer: Capt. William R. Gould
Liaison Officer: Lt. Col. Edward R. Hagenah
Brigade Surgeon: Capt. Eugene R. Hering, Jr., USN
Brigade Dental Officer: Lt. Comdr. Jack J. Kelly, USN

Headquarters and Service Battalion

(32 officers, 183 enlisted men)
Commanding Officer: Maj. Richard E. Sullivan
Executive Officer: Capt. Samuel Jaskilka (to 18 Aug. 50)
Co. Comdr, Hq. Co: 1st.Lt. Nathaniel F. Mann, Jr.

Detachment, 1st Signal Battalion

(4 officers, 99 enlisted men)
Det. Comdr.: Capt. Earl F. Stanley

Company A, 1st Motor Transport Battalion

(6 officers, 112 enlisted men)
Commanding Officer: Capt. Arthur W Ecklund

Company C, 1st Medical Battalion

(5 officers, 94 enlisted men)
Commanding Officer: Comdr. Robert A. Freyling, USN

Company A, 1st Shore Party Battalion

(12 officers, 213 enlisted men)
Commanding Officer: Maj. William L. Batchelor

Company A, 1st Engineer Battalion

(9 officers, 209 enlisted men)
Commanding Officer: Capt. George W. King

Detachment, 1st Ordnance Battalion

(5 officers, 119 enlisted men)
Det. Comdr.: 1stLt Meyer La Bellman

Company A, 1st Tank Battalion

(9 officers, 173 enlisted men)
Commanding Officer: Capt. Gearl M. English
Plat. Comdr., 1st Plat.: 1st Lt. William D. Pomeroy
Plat. Comdr., 2nd Plat.: 2nd Lt .Robert M. Winter (to 3 Sep 50, WIA);
    2nd Lt. John S. Carson (3 Sept. 50, KIA)
Plat. Comdr., 3rd Plat.: 2nd Lt. Granville G. Sweet

1st Battalion, 11th Marines

(44 officers, 474 enlisted men)
Commanding Officer: Lt. Col. Ransom M. Wood
Executive Officer: Maj. Francis R. Schlesinger

Headquarters Battery:

Commanding Officer: Capt. James W. Brayshay

Service Battery:

Commanding Officer: 1st. Lt. Kenneth H. Quelch

Battery A:

Commanding Officer: Capt. James D. Jordan

Battery B:

Commanding Officer: Capt. Arnold C. Hofstetter

Battery C:

Commanding Officer: Capt. William J. Nichols, Jr.

Detachment, 1st Service Battalion

(11 officers, 161 enlisted men)
Det. Comdr.: Capt. Thomas M. Sagar

Detachment, 1st Combat Service Group

(5 officers, 104 enlisted men)
Det. Comdr.: Maj. Thomas J. O'Mahoney

Detachment, Reconnaissance Company

(2 officers, 37 enlisted men)
Det. Comdr.: Capt. Kenneth J. Houghton

Detachment, Military Police Company

(2 officers, 36 enlisted men)
Det. Comdr.: 1s Lt. Nye G. Rodes

1st Amphibian Tractor Company

(10 officers, 244 enlisted men)
Commanding Officer: Maj. James P. Treadwell

1st Amphibian Truck Platoon

(1 officer, 75 enlisted men)
Commanding Officer: 1st. Lt. James E. Condra

VMO-6

Commanding Officer: Maj. Vincent J. Gottschalk

5th Marine Regiment

(132 officers, 2,452 enlisted men)
Commanding Officer: Lt. Col. Raymond L. Murray
Executive Officer: Lt. Col. Lawrence C. Hays, Jr.
S-1: 1st. Lt. Alton C. Weed
S-2: Maj. William C. Esterline
S-3: Lt. Col. George F. Waters, Jr. (to 29 Aug. 50); Maj. Charles H. Brush, Jr.
S-4: Maj. Harold Wallace

Special Staff, 5th Marines:

Chaplain: Lt. Comdr. Orlando Ingvolstad, Jr., USN
Medical Officer: Lt. (jg) William E. Larsen, USN (to 11 Aug. 50); Lt. Comdr. Byron D. Casteel
Supply Officer: Capt. John V. Huff
Motor Transport Officer: Capt. William F. A. Trax (to 15 Aug. 50); 1st Lt. James O. Alison
Ordnance Officer: CWO Bill E. Parrish
Disbursing Officer: Capt. Kenneth L. Shaw
Communications Officer: Maj. Kenneth B. Boyd
Naval Gunfire Officer: Lt. Jerry C. Ragon, USN
Air Officer: 1st Lt. Leo R. Jillisky

1st Battalion, 5th Marines:

Commanding Officer: Lt. Col. George R. Newton
Executive Officer: Maj. Merlin R. Olson
Commanding Officer, H&S Company: Capt. Walter E. Godenius
Commanding Officer, Company A: Capt. John R. Stevens
Commanding Officer, Company B: Capt. John L. Tobin (to 17 Aug. 50, WIA); Capt. Francis I. Fenton, Jr.
Commanding Officer, Weapons Company: Maj. John W. Russell

2nd Battalion, 5th Marines:

Commanding Officer: Lt. Col. Harold S. Roise
Executive Officer: Lt. Col. John W. Stevens II
Commanding Officer, H&S Company: 1st. Lt. David W. Walsh
Commanding Officer, Company D: Capt. John Finn, Jr. (to 8 Aug. 50, WIA); Capt. Andrew M. Zimmer (to 17 Aug. 50, WIA); 1st Lt. Robert T. Hanifin, Jr. (to 22 Aug. 50); 1st Lt. H. J. Smith
Commanding Officer, Company E: Capt. George E. Kittredge (to 7 Aug. 50, WIA); 1st. Lt. William E. Sweeney (to 18 Aug. 50); Capt. Samuel Jaskilka
Commanding Officer, Weapons Company: Maj. Walter Gall (to 10 Aug. 50); Maj. Theodore F. Spiker

3rd Battalion, 5th Marines:

Commanding Officer: Lt. Col. Robert D. Taplett
Executive Officer: Maj. John J. Canney
Commanding Officer, H&S Company: 1st. Lt Arthur E. House, Jr. (to 22 Aug. 50); 1st Lt. Harold D. Fredericks
Commanding Officer, Company G: 1st Lt. Robert D. Bohn
Commanding Officer, Company H: Capt. Joseph C. Fegan, Jr. (to 18 Aug. 50, WIA); Capt. Patrick E. Wildman
Commanding Officer, Weapons Company: Capt. Patrick E. Wildman (to 19 Aug. 50); Maj. Murray Ehrlich

FORWARD ECHELON, 1ST MARINE AIRCRAFT WING

Commanding General: BrigGen Thomas J. Cushman
Chief of Staff: Col Kenneth H. Weir

Marine Aircraft Group 33:

Commanding Officer: Col. Allen C. Koonce (to 20 Aug. 50); Col. Frank G. Dailey
Deputy Commander: Lt. Col. Norman J. Anderson
Executive Officer: Lt. Col. Radford C. West
Commanding Officer, VMF-214: LtCol Walter E. Lischeid
Commanding Officer, VMF-323: Maj. Arnold A. Lund
Commanding Officer, VMF(N)-513: Maj. Joseph H. Reinburg
Commanding Officer, Hq Squadron: Capt. Norman D. Glenn
Commanding Officer, Service Squadron: Lt. Col. James C. Lindsay
Commanding Officer, MTACS-2: Maj. Christian C. Lee

Appendix B

Documents

Staff Study, 4 August Counterattack Plan

Source: EUSAK War Diary

Staff Study
4 Aug   G-3 Plans   to G–3
1. It is believed that EUSAK will be in a position to assume the offensive in the near future. From information currently available reinforced units are due as follows–

2d Division Closes 12 August (1 RCT – 5 Aug).

6th Tank Battalion 15 August

70th Tank Battalion 15 August

73d Tank Battalion 15 August

Considering the service type units due to arrive during the same period it would appear that the most desirable date would fall between the 15th and 20th of August. However, with the movement of the 25th Division into the SAMNANGJU–MUSAN area the arrival of the 5th and the Provisional Marine Brigade sufficient force is at hand to attack between the 5th and 10th of August.

Target date 15 to 20 August.

Advantages:

a.   This would permit the use of a fresh division in the attack.

b.   It would permit the withdrawal of the 24th Division from active combat with the view of giving it much needed rest and rehabilitation and resupply.

c.   It would make available a much larger armored force.

d.   It would be rapidly supported.

Disadvantages:

a.   It would give the enemy time to rest reorganize and generally recover from a long offensive campaign.

b.   It would permit him to shift his units to meet the attack.

c.   The wet season would be well advanced by this time with an excellent chance that water would be high in the rivers.

Target date 5 to 10 August:

Advantages:

a.   It would catch the enemy off balance before he could regroup with an excellent chance of breaking through his shell.

b.   It would be undertaken much earlier in the rainy season.

c.   It would take advantage of his feature.

d.   It would assure the services of the Marine Brigade.

Disadvantages:

a.   Due to lack of service troops supply would be far more difficult.

b.   The attack would be launched with relatively tired and depleted divisions.

c.   The EUSAK reserve would be small.

d.   The Armored units would be extremely limited.

2. It is believed that the main effort should be launch along the axis MASAN–CHINJU–SUCHON–CHONJU, with a holding attack in the area of the 14th Division and a secondary attack along the axis TAEGU–KUMCHON–TAEJON–CHONAN. ROK forces would support by attacking in their area (See Tab A.)

The forces involved would be from South to North.

a.   Task Force:

25th Division

Provisional Marine Brigade

5th Infantry RCT.

b.   24th Divison

c.   1st Cav Division

d.   ROK Forces.

The advantages of this plan are:

a.   That the task force in the south has an excellent chance of cutting off NK forces in the MOKPO–KWANGJU–SUCHON area and relieving pressure in the area of the 24th division relieving that division for other employment in other areas.

b.   The task forces would approach over an excellent road net.

c.   By securing YOSU a roadway is available for an MSR.

d.   In emergency this force could be supplied via IST from the west coast.

e.   It avoids the difficult hill mass to the north.

f.   The division on the Axis TAEGU, YONGDONG, TAEJON, CHONAN would have a double tracked railroad which by reason of its duel construction make repair easier.

g.   The two MSRs converge at TAEJON making it possible to abandon the RR out of YOSU after arrival there.

h.   If the situation requires the southern task force may be turned north east, at NANWAN or CHONJU or TAEJON to relieve resistance in front of the 1st Cavalry.

Disadvantages:

a.   The wide sweep of the task force unless rapidly conducted may put that force in an embarrassing position particularly if the advance of the 1st Cavalry is delayed.

b.   Support of the two widely separated attacks offers some difficulty.

c.   The attack by the 1st Cav Div is down to a narrow corridor and up the NK MSR.

3. Two other courses are considered and discussed:

a.   The main highway through TAEGU, HAMCHANG, CHUNGJU, SEOUI. This was discarded as the demand for services type troops for the support beyond those available in the near future.

b. The highway and railroad north through YONGCHON, UISONG, ANDONG, YONGJU–TANGYANG, WONJU, SEOUL was discarded because of the difficult ground north of YONGJU, the lack of sufficient service type troops and the difficulty of repairing a single tracked railroad.

4. It is recommended that a target date of 5–10 August be accepted and that the plan as indicated in Tab A be undertaken.

STAFF STUDY, 4 AUGUST COUNTERATTACK PLAN

Source: EUSAK War Diaries

Counterattack
1   4 Aug 50   G–3 to C/S

1. For a counterattack to be launched along the MASAN, CHINJU, HODANG axis the following units are immediately available for the formation of a Task Force:

25th Infantry Division

1st Provisional Marine

Brigade

5th Infantry RCT

14th Engineers

1 Truck Company

55 Treadway bridge Co.

2. It is believed that such a force could launch such an attack on or after 7 Aug 50.

3. The Marine Brigade reinforced by the 5th RCT presents a compact organization that is complete within itself and is believed adequate for the initial force in the attack, in the narrow corridor between the mountains and the sea. This not only opens the attack with fresh troops but leaves a more than adequate reserve to support the initial attack, but also to counter-attack such forces as the enemy can currently be moved down from the north without denuding other sectors. In this connection present indications are that the 23rd Infantry and the 78th Tank Bn will be available in the area after the 10th August.

4. Tactical air force is available to support the advance and to attack troops moving from the north against the right flank of the attack, in addition to the Wing of Marine Air that is part of the Marine Brigade. Coordination between the Marine Wing and requirements of the Task Force Commander can best be handled directly between FEAF and those commanders with assistance from this Hqs.

5. Attacks by the ROK forces preceding 7 Aug would tend to hold NK troops in that area. Demonstrations in the area of the 1st Cav Div and the 24th Inf Div could be conducted although there is some doubt as to their effectiveness under present conditions.

6. This force should experience no difficulty in securing CHINJU, and although there is some danger in extending the right flank by an advance to HADONG of committing the entire 25th Div in counterattacks against infiltration or columns from the north, the Army reserve is still increasing. In addition Red troops moving from the north will of necessity come from in front of the 24th Div or 1st Cav Div which may permit launching of limited counterattacks in those areas.

1. [Enclosure]

ETA of Units.

TREACY   BARTLETT

Scotch 638   Scotch 603

Brigadier General E. A. Craig letter to Lieutenant General
Lemuel C. Shepherd, 6 August 1950

Source: Files of Headquarters, Marine Corps, Administrative Division; NARA 127/
E162/Box 29.

Headquarters
1st Provisional Marine Brigade (Reinf), FMF
c/o FPO, San Francisco, California

CONFIDENTIAL   6 Aug 1950

LtGen Lemuel C. Shepherd, USMC
Hq, Fleet Marine Force, Pacific
c/o FPO, San Francisco, California

Dear General Shepherd:

Since my last letter on 20 July the Brigade has been ordered
to EUSAK and arrived in Korea on 2 August for combat employment.
Orders from General MacArthur indicated that the Brigade would be
returned to Kobe, Japan to rejoin the 1st Marine Division at a later date.

Immediately after receipt of verbal orders to proceed to
Korea, I flew with General Cushman and members of my staff to
Taegu, Korea where I reported to General Walker for duty. After
conferences with 8th Army Headquarters and 5th Air Force
Headquarters, General Cushman returned to Japan with orders from
me as to his responsibilities, a copy of these instructions has been
sent to CG, FMFPac.

After spending about 4 days at 8th Army Headquarters I
proceeded to Pusan, Korea to make arrangements for the reception
of the Brigade. During the entire time while at 8th Army Headquarters
the situation was changing hourly with 8th Army elements executing
withdrawal action. It was initially planned by 8th Army Headquarters

that the Brigade would be employed, with the Army 5th Infantry RCT attached, on the south flank to meet the ever-increasing pressure in that area. Inasmuch as the Brigade did not arrive until 2 August it was necessary before that time for the 8th Army to employ the 25th Division in the execution of delaying enemy forces on the south flank. At the present time the Army 5th Infantry is attached to the 25th Infantry Division.

The Brigade arrived in Pusan with the last ship docking at 2130, 2 August. Orders were received from 8th Army at about midnight to move to the vicinity of Ohangwon, which is about 30 miles west of Pusan, in EUSAK reserve. The Brigade commenced movement by motor and train to assigned area at 0600, 3 August and all elements of the Brigade except miscellaneous service elements were in assembly area by 1630, 4 August. Remaining elements were in the area by the morning of 5 August.

A detachment of Combat Service Group has been ordered to remain in Pusan to care for bulk supplies of the Brigade, certain equipment not necessary for employment in this area, personal effects and other rear echelon matters; this detachment consisting of about 140 officers and enlisted. Rations, all PX supplies and ammunition have been pooled with 8th Army supplies on order of 8th Army. In the future these will be provided by 8th Army. 42 2½-ton trucks were provided by 8th Army to assist in making the combination rail and motor movement to assigned bivouac. These trucks, less drivers, remain temporarily attached to the Brigade. It is noted that the Army is extending every help and cooperation within their capabilities that could possibly be expected in their relations with the Brigade.

On arrival in assigned area the Brigade occupied its position tactically and disposed its forces in readiness for combat. Emphasis has been placed on the habitual occupation of high ground and remaining outside of native towns. Terrain characteristics make this difficult, however.

The Air Support Control Section of the Forward Echelon, 1st marine Aircraft Wing landed in Pusan yesterday. This section is proceeding by rail transportation to Brigade headquarters this date.

Every effort is being exerted to ensure that marine air will support marine ground forces when committed to combat. All Army headquarters have assured me that this will be done. VMO-6 was flown to Pusan from Japan. These aircraft have been invaluable in reconnaissance and the helicopters are a Godsend in this type terrain, not only for reconnaissance but for supporting of combat patrols in mountainous terrain; for supply of food, water and ammunition; and the evacuation of casualties. One combat patrol has been thus supported by the Brigade. By separate dispatch to you, 041805, a request has been made to bring out elements of the Helicopter Transport Squadron. It is believed that this innovation will meet with outstanding results in combat in this mountainous terrain for the landing of patrols on top of mountain ranges. Yesterday I sent out one combat patrol to destroy an enemy located by the Brigade reconnaissance elements on extremely high ground. A platoon from the 5th Marines made a torturous 5-mile climb in 2 hours to find that the enemy had evacuated the position. Six men were overcome by heat exhaustion in making this climb and had to be evacuated by helicopter. The transport helicopter will be invaluable in transporting, supply and evacuation of personnel in this type operation inasmuch the helicopters presently available have been invaluable beyond expression. We have only four of the HO3S and I fear they will not be able to sustain all the demands.

The Amphibian Tractor Company was being held at Pusan by 8th Army awaiting a decision from higher authority as to its disposition. 8th Army is extremely concerned about the supply across the Naktong River, just west of Pusan, if the enemy should penetrate farther east and the bridges should be blown across the unfordable Naktong River. Amphibian tractors would be essential for the maintenance of supplies to friendly elements west of the river. The Amphibian Tractor company at last reports left for Japan before 8th Army could obtain a decision on the matter.

By separate dispatch a request has been made for the provision of replacements prior to the arrival of the 1st Marine Division.

Due to the situation (we enter combat at 1500 today) and the fact that a third company is urgently needed, it is recommended that replacements be provided prior to arrival of the 1st Marine Division.

I find that my executive staff is too shorthanded to continue to properly perform their functions on a 24-hour basis. This is true now while we have not been committed to action and will be more acute when we are committed. Assistance is necessary to prevent undue fatigue and resultant loss of efficiency. Request has been made for the augmentation necessary in my 050105 and I consider the augmentation most essential.

Some thought was given by EUSAK to assigning an Army RCT to the Brigade. However, yesterday I was requested to report to CG, 25th Division for a conference at Masan. At the conference, attended by LtGen Walker, MajGen Kean (CG, 25th Div) and myself plus staff members, it developed that the Brigade would be assigned for operations to the 25th Division and that we would take part in an operation to seize and secure the Sachon-Chinju area. The Brigade started moving into the battle position at 0900 this morning. 2/5 marines initially to relieve 1/27 Army on the line by 1500 and to await H-hour expected to be 0700 on 7 August. Division Order was received at 0700 this morning. TACRON is moving to Chinhae to set up to attack through an area where our forces have been stopped and thrown back so far in this war, but am sure we will succeed. I hope that by the time you receive this letter that you will have good news of our action.

There have been no major difficulties encountered by the Brigade. Cooperation by the Army has been extremely favorable. I will continue to keep you advised periodically of the situation of this Brigade.

With kindest personal regards,

E. A. CRAIG,
Brigadier General, U. S. Marine Corps.

LIEUTENANT GENERAL LEMUEL C. SHEPHERD'S CABLE OF 13 AUGUST
1950 TO COMMANDANT OF THE MARINE CORPS ON MARINE HELICOPTERS

Source: COMGENFMFPAC 122230Z Aug 50

NAVAL MESSAGE   NAVY DEPARTMENT

From   COMGENFMFPAC   Action   COMDT MARCORPS

Released By

Date   13 Aug 1950

Reports from Korea indicate that limited number of small helicopters available there are proving of great usefulness in reconnaissance of difficult mountain terrain which exhausts flank patrols. Further consider that were troop carrying type available they would increase greatly the ability of troops to advance rapidly by providing transportation for swift movement of flank security elements from 1 key terrain locality to the next. Accordingly recommend deployment of maximum available helicopter force FECOM earliest. Consider the unequalled opportunity to make significant contribution while at same time demonstration marine foresight and initiative.

SECRET
122230Z

Appendix C
Citations

Source: Montross, Lynn and Nicholas A. Canzona. *U.S. Marine Operations in Korea. Vol. 1, The Pusan Perimeter.* Washington: Historical Branch, G-3, Marine Corps, 1954.

September 29, 1950
PRESIDENTIAL UNIT CITATION
The President of the Republic of Korea takes profound pleasure in citing for outstanding and heroic performance of duty on the field of battle during the period 2 August 1950–6 September 1950.
THE FIRST UNITED STATES PROVISIONAL MARINE BRIGADE for the Award of THE PRESIDENTIAL UNIT CITATION

The First United States Provisional Marine Brigade was a vital element in the first major counterattack against the enemy.

In late July and early August 1950, the enemy had swept through the Chulla Provinces and had rapidly approached along the South Korean coast to a point only 35 miles from the vital port of Pusan. Together with the 25th Infantry Division, the First United States Provisional Marine Brigade, from 7 August to 12 August 1950, played a major role in attacking and driving back the enemy.

During the period 17 August to 20 August 1950 in conjunction with the 24th Infantry Division and units of the 2d Infantry Division, the First United States Provisional Marine Brigade attacked a great pocket of enemy forces who had successfully crossed the Naktong River and established a firm beachhead on the eastern bank. The Brigade attacked with such determination and skill as to earn the admiration of all who saw or knew of its battle conduct.

Later, on the night of 31 August–1 September, the enemy again launched an all-out offensive against the United Nations Forces. The First United States Provisional Marine Brigade was in Army reserve at that time. With the 2d Infantry Division, the Brigade again was committed in almost the same area of its earlier action against the Naktong pocket in the neighborhood of Yongsan. Again the gallant Marine forces were instrumental in preventing the enemy from capturing their objective and cutting the north-south lines of communication of the United Nations Forces.

The brilliant performance of duty in combat in Korea of each individual of the First United States Provisional Marine Brigade is in accord with the highest traditions of the military service.

This citation carries with it the right to wear the Presidential Unit Citation Ribbon by each individual of the First United States Provisional Marine Brigade which served in Korea in the stated period.

(Signed) SYNGMAN RHEE

THE SECRETARY OF THE NAVY
WASHINGTON
The President of the United States takes pleasure in presenting the
PRESIDENTIAL UNIT CITATION to the FIRST PROVISIONAL
MARINE BRIGADE, REINFORCED
for service as set forth in the following CITATION:

"For extraordinary heroism in action against enemy aggressor forces in Korea from 7 August to 7 September 1950. Functioning as a mobile, self-contained, air-ground team, the First Provisional Marine Brigade, Reinforced, rendered invaluable service during the fierce struggle to maintain the foothold established by friendly forces in the Pusan area during the early stages of the Korean conflict. Quickly moving into action as numerically superior enemy forces neared the Naktong River on the central front and penetrated to within 35 miles of Pusan in the southern sector, threatening the integrity of the entire defensive perimeter, this hard-hitting, indomitable team counterattacked serious enemy penetrations at three different points in rapid succession. Undeterred by roadblocks, heavy hostile automatic weapons and highly effective artillery fire, extremely difficult terrain and intense heat, the Brigade met the invaders with relentless determination and, on each crucial occasion, hurled them back in disorderly retreat. By combining sheer resolution and esprit de corps with sound infantry tactics and splendid close air support, the Brigade was largely instrumental in restoring the line of defense, in inflicting thousands of casualties upon the enemy and in seizing large amounts of ammunition, equipment and other supplies. The brilliant record achieved by the unit during the critical early days of the Korean conflict attests to the individual valor and competence of the officers and men and reflects the highest credit upon the First Provisional Marine Brigade, Reinforced, and the United States Naval Service."

All of the First Provisional Marine Brigade except the First Amphibian Tractor Company participated in operations against enemy aggressor forces in Korea from 7 August to 7 September 1950.

The following reinforcing units of the First Provisional Marine Brigade participated in operations against enemy aggressor forces in Korea from 7 August to 7 September 1950:

Forward Echelon, First Marine Aircraft Wing (less ground personnel)
Marine Air Group Thirty-Three, Reinforced (less ground personnel)
Marine Observation Squadron Six plus Helicopter Section, Head
    quarters Squadron
Air Support Section of Marine Tactical Air Control Squadron Two
United States Army: Counter Intelligence Corps and Military
Intelligence Special Detachment personnel attached to the
Headquarters Company, Headquarters and Service Battalion,
First Provisional Marine Brigade.

    For the President,
    (Signed) R. A. ANDERSON
    Secretary of the Navy

NOTES

PREFACE AND ACKNOWLEDGMENTS

1. Estes, *Marines Under Armor*.
2. Fehrenbach, *This Kind of War*, 142.
3. Montross, *The Pusan Perimeter*, 259.
4. Alexander, *Korea*, 124, 131.
5. Blair, *The Forgotten War*, 193.
6. Sloan, *The Darkest Summer*; rather something of a polemic. Millett, *The War for Korea*; includes an important revision on U.S. and South Korean Army performance in July-September 1950, but restates official history on the marine brigade. Hammes, *Forgotten Warriors*; steeped in presentism.

1. THE MARINE CORPS AND THE KOREAN CRISIS OF 1950

1. American Consul Tripoli message 241357ZJun50 and Chief of Naval Operations (CNO) 031638ZJun50 (hereafter, date/24-hour time/time zone/ month/year of message release: 03/1638/Z [meaning GMT]/June/1950 in this case); National Archives and Records Administration (NARA), Washington, D.C., Record Group 127, Entry 162, Box 10 (hereafter RG127/E162/10).
2. Newton biographical file, Reference Section, Marine Corps Historical Division, Marine Corps University, Quantico, VA (hereafter RefSect).
3. Allison, "Black Sheep Squadron," 416. Exercise data from NARA RG127/E18b/1083, 1098.
4. Ross, *American War Plans*, 49, 67–70, 88–90.
5. Ibid., 114–17.
6. Millett, *Semper Fidelis*, 457–64,469–74. The standard account is by Keiser, *The U.S. Marine Corps and Defense Unification*.

7. *The Marine Corps Reserve*, 137, cited in Allison, "Black Sheep Squadron," 401.

8. Allison, "Black Sheep Squadron," 419; Dyer oral history interview, 238.

9. Memo Director Plans and Programs to CMC 12May50, RG127/E162/40.

10. 1st Marine Division (hereafter 1st MarDiv) Quarterly Readiness Report noting also "Shortage of personnel in light of recent developments," 10Jul50; RG127/E162/30.

11. Chart, "Marine Squadron Operational Readiness" March 1950, RG127/E162/30.

12. Memo Army DC/S Administration memo for CNO 23Feb49; RG127/E162/2.

13. Memo Bureau of Ordnance to Army DC/S Admin, 15Mar50, RG127/E162/2.

14. Until declassified documents of the USSR became available, the decision-making for the invasion of June 1950 remained more obscure. The earlier works revealing this information include Kathryn Weathersby, "New Russian Documents on the Korean War," *Cold War International History Project Bulletin* nos. 6–7 (Winter 1995–1996): 30–84; "To Attack or Not to Attack? Stalin, Kim Il Sung, and the Prelude to War," (Spring 1995): 1–9, and "The Soviet Role in the Early Phase of the Korean War: New Documentary Evidence," *Journal of American-East Asian Relations* 2, no. 4 (Winter 1993): 425–58. The growing literature on the origins of the Korean War is best assessed by beginning with Millett, *The War for Korea.*

15. Army historian Roy E. Appleman cited thirty tanks joining the 7th Division just before it crossed the parallel. This gave North Korea a total of 150 Soviet-built T-34 tanks committed in June 1950. However, a key weakness of the KPA remained its artillery strength, limited to the doctrinal divisional artillery of a Soviet infantry division. But Soviet doctrine provided for considerable reinforcing artillery for use in offensive operations, and these were not to be found in the North Korean order of battle. Appleman, *South to the Naktong,* 10.

16. Ibid., 35n.

17. Ibid., 37.

18. Ibid., 38–48, passim.

19. Montross, *The Pusan Perimeter,* 48–49.

20. CINCPACFLT 020949Z Jul50; CNO 021621Jul50, RefSect; also in RG127/E162/10.

21. CINCPACFLT 041031Z Jul50; CNO 032224Z and 041912Z Jul50, RefSect; also in RG127/E162/10; Lt. Gen. Shepherd's initial table of organization for the brigade is FMFPac OpPlan 2–50, 5Jul50, Quantico, Marine Corps University, GRC Archive, Korea File, Box 1, Folder 2.

22. Shepherd, "Korean War Diary 2 July to 7 December 1950," 3-5 (hereafter ShepDiary).

23. CG FMFPAC 050101 Jul50, and CG 1stMarDiv 061805Z Jul50; RG127/E162/10; CMC 051730Z Jul50, RG127/E162/36. Shepherd's original scheme is FMFPac Op Plan 2–50, 5Jul50; Gray Research Center Archives

(hereafter GRC), Quantico, Korea File, Box 1, Folder 2; 1stProvBrig Special Action Report (hereafter SAR) 2Aug-6Sep50, 2 confirms CNO reconsidered the request for the rifle platoons and approved it, this would have been most likely the result of Cates's recommendations. ShepDiary, 6–7. Craig, "Incidents of Service 1917–1951" typescript, including a twelve-page extract from field notebook, Korea, 154–55 (hereafter, "Incidents)." Copy in author possession, others held by individuals, one on file at Marine Corps Recruit Depot Command Museum, San Diego. The SARs are now available in digitized form at the GRC Archives, Marine Corps University, Quantico, and on paper in NARA RG127.

24. O.P. Smith "Aide-Memoire—Korea 1950–51" RefSect, Korea Files, (hereafter Smith A-M).

25. Montross, *The Pusan Perimeter,* 49

26. CINCFE 070309Z Jul50, RG127/E162/10

27. CG 1st MarDiv 031931Z Jul50, RG127/E162/10; CMC 041901Z and 110513Z Jul50, ibid., Box 36.

28. On Stuart, see my *Marines Under Armor,* 93–138 passim; memo is RG127/E162/11.

29. Deployment of 6th, 70th, and 73rd Tank Battalions by Fourth, Second, and Third Armies, respectively, ordered by three telexes of Movement Control Branch, G-4; Army 110530ZJul50 on 2nd Infantry Division; CINCFE 132013ZJul50 on RCT 5; RG127/E162/10.

30. CINCFE 130553ZJul50 RG127/E162/10. Curiously, the first marine corps reinforcement identified for the Far East was a 90mm antiaircraft artillery battalion for Yokosuka Naval Base requested by CINCFE in April and approved by JCS, discussed in CINCFE 170257ZJun50, and later accelerated when the war broke out; RG127/E162/10.

31. CMC 012035Z and 051622Z Aug50, RG127/E162/36; MC Board report is 19May49 "Project 614: Test of AT rifle grenade Energa," box 20. There remains no evidence that a single AT rifle grenade was fired in anger in this campaign. The Marine Corps Equipment Board reported that the Energa penetrated eight inches of armor sloped at thirty-five degrees, while the current issue M9A1 antitank rifle grenade penetrated only four inches and the 2.36-inch rocket launcher only 3.5 inches of sloped plating.

32. CMC 142037Z Jul50, RG127/E162/36; CMC 121548ZJul50 to All MarCor; On August 17 (CG, 1MarBde 170130ZAug50), the brigade would report 5th Marines under strength by sixteen officers and four hundred enlisted men, mostly in infantry specialties; RG127/E162/11.

33. Commander Fleet Air, Atlantic (hereafter ComAirLant) 302201Z Jun50, CNO 121912Z Jul50, and 021631Z Aug50; RG127/E162/10.

34. Sailing measures and schedules include CNO 301804Z Jun50, CINCPacFlt 112015ZJul50 and ComCarDiv 5 030545ZZJul50; RG127/E162/10; sabotage warnings are CNO 211934ZJul50 and 051731ZAug50, ComPhibGroup 1 020952ZJul50 in RG127/E162/10 and CMC 191740ZJul50, Box 36.

35. Telcon CNO and ComPacFlt 5Jul50, RG127/E162/11; Appleman, *South to the Naktong,* 120.

36. The message is CINCFE 250715ZJul50, RG127/E162/10.

37. Field, *History of United States Naval Operations Korea*, 85.

38. The slower LSDs, laden with tanks and amtracs, departed on the earlier date. Operational report, A Company 1st Tank Battalion, 5th Marines SAR 2 August–6 September 1950. CMC 051730ZJul50 ordered the Pacific Department of the Marine Corps to furnish personnel not available at Camp Pendleton for use in forming the additional rifle platoons RG127/E162/36

39. Montross, *The Pusan Perimeter*, 54.

40. Chapin, *Fire Brigade*, 8.

41. Thanks to Allan R. Millett for indirectly tipping me to the lack of World War II combat experience in 1st Marine Division ground field grade officers. The bulk of the officer biographical data may be found in individual biographical files, RefSect.

42. Craig oral history interview; cited in Craig's obituary by marine corps oral historian, Benis M. Frank, "General Craig's Father Warned Him about the Marines," *Fortitudine* (Fall 1995): 14.

43. Koonce went to the air staff of FMFPac. MAG-33 Hist Diary SAR Aug50.

44. Lischeid was shot down and killed in action 25 Sept 1950.

45. Hal Roise is featured in the otherwise polemical Henry Berry, *Hey Mac, Where Ya Been*, 56–66.

46. He apparently had always wanted to change to the infantry and in the 5th Marines was given command of a rifle company; Fegan oral history interview, 74, 90, 94.

47. MAG-33 SAR; VMF-214 was cruising on board the escort carrier deploying to Korea from the West Coast, an obvious choice as it was the more ready squadron.

48. Some secondary sources persist in stating the F7F night fighter was employed at this time, but it entered service later, with the 1st MAW deployment; MAG-33 SAR, Logistics Annex F.

49. Interview with Donald R. Gagnon, also in Oscar Gilbert, *Marine Corps Tank Battles in Korea*, 16–18; SAR A Company 1st Tank Battalion, Annex Fox to SAR of 5th Marines 2 Aug–6Sept50. USS *Fort Marion* carried fourteen tanks, another thirteen rode USS *Gunston Hall*; ComPhibPac 131643Z Jul50 to CG 1st Bde: "Do not intend Ft Marion turn back. Key repair pts ship in APD 124 [destroyer transport USS] *H A Buss* if practicable for xfr at sea to *Ft Marion*." Ft Marion 131925ZJul50; ComPhibPac to ComPacFlt 141833ZJul50; RG127/E162/Box11.

50. Craig, "Incidents," 155–58; curiously Stratemeyer's diary has no mention of the meeting, cf. Y'Blood, *The Three Wars of Lt. Gen George E. Stratemeyer* (hereafter Stratemeyer diary), 81n.

2. FIRST FORTNIGHT IN KOREA

1. Craig "Incidents," 179; General Shepherd's "diary" contains no entries between 27 July and 13 August 1950, at least in the typescript version he sent to the director, USMC Historical Division, on 24 June 1974; one can

only await access to Shepherd's complete personal diary and that of his assistant chief of staff for operations, Krulak, with evident interest.

2. Appleman, *South to the Naktong*, chapters 8–18. Historical sketches of the units of the North Korean Army, or Korean People's Army (KPA), may be found in U.S. Far East Command, *History of the North Korean Army* (31 July 1952).

3. Appleman, *South to the Naktong*, 247.

4. Chandler, *Papers of Dwight David Eisenhower* , 2467, 2599. From such a background Walker could only be expected to order a more aggressive posture as his troops crossed the Naktong to take up final defense positions of the Pusan Perimeter. Walker quote in Appleman, *South to the Naktong*, 252.

5. Staff Study, 4 August G-3 Plans to G-3, EUSAK War Diary (hereafter EUSAK WD) RG407/E429/1091; copy in appendix of this book.

6. Appleman, *South to the Naktong*, 258; Munroe, *Second United States Infantry Division in Korea*, 3–4. EUSAK WD entries for 1 Aug show 2nd Infantry Division strength is 3,497, and show RCT 9 had reported for operations; RG407/E429/Box1090. One of the more recent authors to claim the marine brigade arrived first from the United States is Ron Brown, *A Few Good Men*, 207.

7. 5th Marines SAR 2 Aug–6Sep50, 3; quotations from Crag interview, 164; Craig's "Incidents" appear to have this event excised from the reproduced and circulated copies, and he included no extract for this day from his field notebook in the appendix; CG 1st Marine Bde 021348ZAug50 reported arrival of ships carrying the non-aviation units of the brigade at Pusan 020817Z, less dock landing ship USS *Gunston Hall*, which had detached to take the amphibian tractor company and amphibious truck platoon to Kobe; RG127/E162/11.

8. See Taplett, *Dark Horse Six*, 22; this slightly longer quote appeared in Taplett's original manuscript, author files.

9. Craig interview, 162. All times are local.

10. EUSAK WD 30Jul50 RG407/E429/1087

11. Appleman, *South to the Naktong*, 257.

12. Ibid., 259–61.

13. Ibid., 261–65.

14. Craig interview, 167; 5th Marines SAR.

15. *Library of Congress Country Studies*, http://lcweb2.loc.gov/frd/cs/krtoc.html; *CIA Factbook*, https://www.cia.gov/library/publications/the-world-factbook/. Fans of the Summer Olympics will recall the deliberate scheduling of the 1988 games in late September, vice the harsh August of South Korea.

16. MAG-33 SAR, Ops summary; Logistics Annex F.

17. Ibid.

18. MAG-33 SAR Communications Annex E.

19. Field, *History of United States Naval Operations Korea*, 129–30, 134; VMF-214 SAR Aug50.

20. Citation to Reusser's gold star in lieu of second award of the Navy Cross, approved on 3 May 1951; Awards Branch, HQMC Quantico, Korea-NC Files (hereafter Awards Section files).

21. Field, *History of United States Naval Operations Korea*, 141–43.

22. VMF-214 SAR Aug50.

23. VMF-214 SAR Sep50; VMF-323 SAR 3Aug-6Sep50.

24. VMF-323 SAR Aug50.

25. VMF-323 SAR 3Aug–6Sep50, 5; VMF-214 SAR August50. As already observed above, the night fighter squadron remained under 5th Air Force control for the entire period.

26. VMO-6 SAR 2 August-6 Sept50.

27. EUSAK WD, 6 and 7 Aug50; RG407/E429/1091-92.

28. Appleman, *South to the Naktong*, 108, 190–95, 270, 486.

29. Drea, *In the Service of the Emperor*, 65–71. Eichelberger remained in command of the Eighth Army until his retirement in 1948. The attention he may have devoted to its combat training during 1946–48 must remain a matter of speculation.

30. EUSAK WD 6 Aug50; in it, the G3 section also reports attaching a "Korean Commando company" to the marine brigade, later appearing in the Eighth Army troop list as the 4th Provisional Security Police Company. RG/E429/1091.

31. Knox, *The Korean War*, 102–103.

32. Although USMC accounts claim excellent use of air drops to resupply the army company and marine platoon on Hill 342, Appleman, *South to the Naktong*, 272, tersely reports that only the third such effort succeeded: "The enemy got the first drop. The second was a mile short of the drop zone."

33. 5th Marines Antitank Company SAR, 2.

34. Navy Cross (Davis) and DSC citations and orders (Batluck, James, and Macy), Awards Section files.

35. Taplett, *Dark Horse Six*, 39.

36. Craig quotations from "Incidents," 182. Fenton's remarks from his oral history interview cited in Knox, 108–10.

37. Montross, *The Pusan Perimeter*, Chapter 7; 5th Marines SAR. By the end of the day, none of Lt. Pomeroy's 1st platoon tanks remained in operation, and the M26s were already showing their mechanical cantankerousness, no doubt made worse by their long storage period in the Barstow Depot. This platoon would remain the "hard-luck" platoon until after the Inchon landings next month, when they finally extracted their revenge. The Army Distinguished Service Cross posthumously awarded to Maj. McNeeley cited his "superb leadership, fearless determination, and extraordinary heroism under fierce battle conditions materially contributed to the successful accomplishment of the 3d Battalion's objective."

38. Appleman, *South to the Naktong*, 281–85.

39. Appleman, *South to the Naktong*, 286.

40. Craig, "Incidents," 162, 183.

41. Fenton, "Changellon Valley," 52. Fenton oral history interview, 31. Fenton's interviews present a telling narrative of combat in Korea as a company commander, more exciting than many novels. Distinguished Service Cross citations for Sowl, Fear, and Budd, Awards Section.

42. EUSAK WD 8 Aug; the figure of one hundred must be considered rounded, i.e., estimated, but gives evidence of the priority being given to the

division. Daily sorties of the air force at this stage of the Pusan campaign ranged 250–350 daily. RG407/E429/1092.

43. Moses casualty card, RefSect; award data from Awards Branch, HQMC, copies in author files, with special mention herein as Moses's exploits never had been noted in secondary sources.

44. VMF-214 and VMF-323 SARs for August 1950.

45. Craig, "Incidents," 184. EUSAK WD personnel summaries reported cumulative losses through 13 August as 29 killed, 249 wounded and 12 non-battle injured. Shepherd's diary, however, noted problems with Eighth Army reporting USMC casualties as army losses. RG407/E429/1093-94.

3. NAKTONG BATTLES

1. Appleman, *South to the Naktong*, 336–50

2. EUSAK WD 11Aug50. RG407/E429/1093.

3. Ibid., 351–363

4. MacArthur chose the 24th Division to go first to Korea because of its proximity to the ports in Japan opposite Korea; by the time the division pulled out of frontline duty, 22 July, it had retreated one hundred miles, suffered 30 percent casualties, including 2,400 missing, among them the commanding general; its effective strength was by then 8,660 men; Robertson, *Counterattack on the Naktong*, 6–8; personnel summaries from EUSAK WD, various dates.

5. Ibid., 13–16; Appleman, *South to the Naktong*, 289–91.

6. Robertson, *Counterattack on the Naktong*, 20.

7. Ibid., 46–57; EUSAK WD 9–12Aug50, RG407/E429/1092-93.

8. EUSAK WD 12Aug50, RG407/E429/1093; Robertson, *Counterattack on the Naktong*, 67–82.

9. EUSAK WD 15August50, RG407/E429/1094. Walker's comment has been much quoted without variation, cited for reference herein as Robertson, 81.

10. SARs 1st and 3rd Battalions, 5th Marines, 1st Battalion, 11th Marines; Craig, "Incidents," 184. Craig also noted the first hot meal, 161.

11. EUSAK WD 15Aug50; on 16 August, the 144 close support sorties were divided 67, 47, 12 and 18, respectively. RG407/E429/1094–95.

12. Robertson, 83–85.

13. 1st Marine Brigade Basic Report, SAR, 12; Robertson, 86–87.

14. Murray oral history interview, 192.

15. Robertson, 88; Montross, *The Pusan Perimeter*, 176–79. There is evident confusion over Cloverleaf Hill in the USMC account, which it places behind the 9th Infantry lines, in its stead labeling the 9th Infantry objective "Finger Hill."

16. SARs 2nd Battalion, 5th Marines, VMF-214, and VMF-323.

17. Crowson DSC citation, Awards Section files.

18. Johnston DSC citation, Ibid. Combat narrative constructed from SARs 1st and 2nd Battalions, 5th Marines, A Company 1st Tank Battalion, 1st Battalion, 11th Marines; Robertson, 88–91; Montross, *The Pusan Perimeter*, 179–192; Appleman, *South to the Naktong*, 310–314.

19. Craig letter to C/S (chief of staff), Army 23Aug50, RG127/E162/33, 40 [2 copies]. Most curiously, the marine corps official history substituted USMC Corsairs for the air force F-51s, and gave them credit for the fourth T-34. Yet neither squadron claimed participation and flights launched from the carriers recovered by 1920 that day. The Antitank Company reported results of its 1st Platoon firing on the three T-34s it engaged: "#1 tank: 6 HEAT, 3 HE; #2 tank: 2 HEAT, 8 HE, 4 WP; #3 tank, 3 HE, 3 WP. Also during this action, one 3.5" rocket launcher team of this organization fired three rounds on each of the first two tanks, but results of the last three rounds couldn't be observed due to smoke and flames." SARs VMF-214, VMF-323, Antitank Company; Montross, *The Pusan Perimeter*, 193–94.

20. Robertson, 92; Coox, "U.S. Armor in the Antitank Role, 19.

21. Knox, *The Korean War*, 150–55.

22. SARs VMF-214, VMF-323, A Company 1st Tank Battalion, 1st Battalion, 11th Marines; EUSAK WD 17–19 Aug50, RG407/E429/1095-96. VMF-214 did not launch its first strike until 1230 that day, so the fighter squadrons had resumed sequential flight operations, perhaps indicating the brigade command sensed the enemy collapse.

23. SARs 3rd Battalion, 5th Marines; Montross, *The Pusan Perimeter*, 206; EUSAK WD entries for 17 and 18 August show 32 killed, 348 wounded; RG407/E429/1092. RG407/E429/1095.

24. 24th Infantry Division War Diary, 19Aug50, RG407/E429/3482; Appleman, *South to the Naktong*, 318; on 26 Aug Gen. Walker ordered the 34th Infantry reduced to "paper" strength, its last men transferred 31 Aug to the 19th and 21st Infantry Divisions as cadre for building third battalions in each; Appleman, *South to the Naktong*, 389.

25. Robertson, 94-96; Lt. Col. Roise noted in his after action report that only his own mortar and tank fire covered his advance and that no artillery close supporting fire was provided; 2nd Battalion, 5th Marines SAR.

26. CG, FMFPac 122230ZAug50, RG127/E162/10.

27. Top secret "eyes only" letter to Gen. Hoyt Vandenberg quoted in Stratemeyer diary entry 23Aug50, 130.

28. Stratemeyer diary, 131–32.

29. Ibid., 132.

30. Ibid., 136.

31. Ibid., 137.

32. Knox, *The Korean War*, 164–67.

33. SARs 5th Marines, 2nd Battalion, 5th Marines, 1st Battalion, 11th Marines. Taplett, in his acerbic autobiographical account, *Dark Horse Six*, 81–82, related during this period his contact with the "34th Infantry [Regiment]" for planning counterattacks (it had already been disbanded, but the 35th Infantry remained nearby), and the return of his seventeen-year-old troops detained in Japan. No records confirm this and the orders of the commandant specifically excluded the brigade from the policy, which did affect the 1st Marine Division. It thus remains a most unreliable—perhaps "induced" —memoir. CMC 181940ZAug50: "Effective this date it is the policy of the commandant that no marine under eighteen years of age will be placed in

combat." But a later message stated that it did not apply to the marine brigade in combat until replacements arrived; RG127/E162/11.

34. Montross, *The Pusan Perimeter*, 209, claims that the full draft of eight hundred arrived, but this seems incorrect because Craig recorded three hundred in his field journal entry on 24 August, and the larger number would have included the missing rifle companies. In addition, the stated "extensive training" these replacements received at Masan appears dubious; Craig, "Incidents," 185–86.

35. Appleman, *South to the Naktong*, 395; later estimates of FEC concluded that the KPA disposed of 97,850 troops on 1 September; EUSAK Op Summary, 3, noted 175,496 U.N. troops present in the perimeter on the same date; RG407/E429/1101.

36. Appleman, *South to the Naktong*, 376–450 passim.

37. Ibid., 443–453.

38. EUSAK Op Summary, 2; RG407/E429/1101.

39. Craig, "Incidents," 187, field notebook entry for 2 September; the EUSAK WD shows the brigade still under Eighth Army vice 2nd Division control until 3 September. RG407/E429/1102.

40. Montross, *The Pusan Perimeter*, 213, discusses the tactical air control detachment being out of touch with Craig, but makes no mention of the location of the aircraft units; SAR VMF-323, Sept50.

41. SAR, MTACS-2.

42. SARs 1st Brigade, 5th Marines, 2nd Battalion, 5th Marines; EUSAK WD 1–3 Sept, Box 1102.

43. Appleman, *South to the Naktong*, 22, 395, 519. The regiment of the KPA 9th Division not committed to the Pusan campaign would later receive its taste of fighting marines against the 1st Marines at Yongdungpo before the Battle of Seoul.

44. Appleman, *South to the Naktong*, 461–63, a curiously sketchy description of the action.

45. Montross, *The Pusan Perimeter*, 217–20; Craig, "Incidents," 164–65, 167–168, 187; Gilbert, *Marine Corps Tank Battles in Korea*, 41–42. Note Montross refers to Hill 116 as 117, but the former is used by the army history and SAR 2nd Battalion, 5th Marines. Winter's silver star citation, Awards Section files.

46. SAR 1st Battalion, 5th Marines.

47. Appleman, *South to the Naktong*, 464; Gilbert, *Marine Corps Tank Battles in Korea*, 42–43.

48. Zwarka DSC citation, Award Section files.

49. Montross, *The Pusan Perimeter*, 219–227; SAR 2nd Battalion, 5th Marines; USMC casualties for the day totaled 34 killed and 157 wounded, Appleman, *South to the Naktong*, 464. Billings DSC citation, Award Section files. Some of these casualties apparently took place when one or more U.S. Army tanks entered the fight near Myong from the north, perhaps responding to aid the army troops engaged earlier in the morning. They instead shot up some of the D Company marines. The incident is not mentioned in either army or marine corps official histories, but rather in later in oral histories,

taken into consideration by Ent, *Fighting on the Brink*, 299–300, 318n. Knox, *The Korean War*, 174–78 passim.

50. SARs 2nd and 3rd Battalions, 5th Marines.

51. Appleman, *South to the Naktong*, 465; SAR 3rd Battalion, 5th Marines.

52. Appleman, *South to the Naktong*, 465; SARs 1st and 3rd Battalions, 5th Marines.

53. SAR 1st Battalion, 5th Marines, Gilbert, *Marine Corps Tank Battles in Korea*, 45–46. I had long pondered the army and USMC official history versions of this tank fight, which assert that two KPA tanks, accompanied by an *armored personnel carrier* (APC), spearheaded this attack. Insofar as the KPA had never used APCs in battle, it remained a curiosity. The answer, for me, came in reading Capt. Fenton's oral history interview of November 1950 wherein he stated that the third tank at the Second Naktong was a camouflaged T-34 that simply appeared to be a halftrack; Fenton interview, 76, cf. his gripping narrative of both Naktong actions as a company commander, 43–47, 69–82. Fenton also remarked on the Energa AT grenade as never being used in combat, but that one did blast a chunk out of an M26, probably referring to attempts to destroy the two M26 tanks left behind at Second Naktong, in the end destroyed by burning.

54. Montross, *The Pusan Perimeter*, 230; SAR 5th Marines; SAR VMF-323.

55. Walker's G-3, Col. John A. Bullock, comment in EUSAK WD 4Sep50 RG407/E429/1102.

56. Craig, "Incidents," 168.

57. Murray interview, 195.

58. SARs VMF-214, VMF-323, 1st Battalion, 11th Marines. On 5 September, Maj. Gen. Keiser relieved Col. Hill as commander of the 9th Infantry.

59. The USAF units brought in from Okinawa were the 51st Fighter-Interceptor Wing comprising the 16th and 25th Fighter-Interceptor Squadrons, all flying relatively short-ranged F-80 jets previously employed in the air defense of the Ryukyu Islands. Appleman, *South to the Naktong*, 543.

4. REORGANIZATION AND RECORDING

1. SAR 5th Marines, but confusion remains, as the brigade's historical diary reports the "completion" of the movement to Pusan on 7 September. Yet the air control squadron did not send the Air Support Section from Chinhae to Pusan until 10 September, SAR, MTACS-2.

2. Craig, "Incidents," 13; Montross, *The Pusan Perimeter*, 238.

3. ShepDiary, 47.

4. MRO Tokyo 110030ZSep50: 1ProvMarBde CP shifts from Pusan to USS *Cavalier* APA 37 effective 110200Z; CG1MarDiv 100802ZSep50: "Effective 13 September 1950, the 1st Provisional Marine Brigade, and its Headquarters and Service Battalion and Headquarters Company are disbanded, BGen Craig resumes duty as assistant division commander 1st Marine Division"; RG127/E162/10. CG, FMFPac letter to CMC 28Sep50 indicated the aviation units had reverted to their parent wing on 6 September 1950 upon the arrival in the area of Maj. Gen. Field Harris and his headquarters,

thus ending any further illusion of the brigade as an air-ground team! RG127/E162/14.

5. September 1950 SARs, VMF-214 and 323.

6. CG, FMFPac 070145ZSep50, with penciled note by unknown marine, perhaps Lt. Col. Stuart: RG127/E162/14.

7. COMNAVFE 091352Z Oct 50 RG127/E162/11. Author's italics in summary that follows.

8. ShepDiary, 29–30.

9. CMC letter 4 Aug 52, Marine Corps Board Study, "An Evaluation of the Influence of Marine Corps Forces on the Course of the Korean War (4 Aug 50–15 Dec 50)," page II-A-9, copy in Marine Corps University, GRC Archive, Korea Files, Box 1, folder 27.

10. Ibid, II-A-17 to 19. NB, even the hallowed claim by the USMC for first use of the helicopter in combat begs refinement, since the same claim emerges from USAF special operations units, citing the case of the 1st Air Commando Group organized on 29 March 1944 from an earlier air force unit created to support a guerrilla force in Burma in early 1943. The unit eventually operated 346 aircraft, including four YR-4 helicopters. They also claim the first to use the helicopter in combat. The U.S. Navy was also operating their own HO3S–1 helicopters in support of carrier task forces engaged in combat operations, principally rescuing aircrew and performing logistics missions.

11. Ibid., II-A-21.

12. Ibid., II-A-22, author italics.

13. Ibid, II-A-26, 27.

14. Ibid., II-A-30.

15. Ibid., II-A-31-35.

16. Montross, *The Pusan Perimeter*, v, 239ff; the staff study was not recognized in the preface to volume 2, although it dealt equally with the Inchon-Seoul operation.

17. Montross, *The Pusan Perimeter*, v.

18. Montross, *The Pusan Perimeter*, 241, cf. 244: "Altogether, the participation of the 1st Provisional Brigade was an important factor in stopping the North Korean invasion in August 1950 and punishing the invaders so severely that they were ripe for a crushing defeat the following month."

19. Montross, *The Pusan Perimeter*, 242–43.

20. SARs VMF-214 and VMF-323.

21. John D. Manza, "A Critical Analysis of the 1st Provisional Marine Brigade Operations in Korea, August–September, 1950" (Quantico: Marine Corps University, 1999), first published as "The First Provisional Marine Brigade in Korea," 2 parts, *Marine Corps Gazette* 84 (July and August 2000), 66–74 and 82–89.

22. Stratemeyer diary, 297. This lesser-known statement requires frequent juxtaposition to MacArthur's statement to Craig in July 1950 that "people say I don't like marines" and his well-publicized quote after Inchon, "I have just returned from visiting the marines at the front, and there is not a finer fighting organization in the world!" Craig, "Incidents," 163.

23. "I had expected that some time would be devoted to the Korean War and what the First Marine Division was doing as they were then in combat. Instead it was a shock to see eight young women Marines in new style uniforms march into the conference room. At great length a discussion was then held as to what changes had been made or should be made in these uniforms. Each woman Marine was in a different outfit so it took some time. After this important matter was attended to a discussion was then held as to whether Marines from Quantico should be required to wear the old style battle jackets on liberty as shirts in summer did not look military. The battle jackets had been non-uniform for some time. However, after a great and lengthy discussion it was decided there were enough jackets at the depot of supplies to outfit these men from Quantico and that they should wear them. It was then that the G-2 and G-3 sections brought in a big map of the Korean area and announced they were ready to give a briefing on the situation in Korea and the Marines in particular. I was delighted to think that I would get the latest dope from Korea. Instead, the senior general announced after looking at his watch that it was 11:45 and time for lunch, and that the briefing on Korea would be delayed until next Friday. This really shook me. I got to my feet and walked out of the room in disgust. I could not believe that such indifference could be real. I felt that justice was not being done to the men in Korea, and that I did not want to be part of the Washington scene. I was probably a little quick on the trigger after what I had gone through in Korea, but when I arrived home that night I told my wife that I was going to turn my suit in. The next day, I sent in my written request for retirement to take effect on or after June 1, 1951." Craig, "Incidents," 174–75.

Craig persisted in his retirement decision over the objections of the commandant and secretary of the navy, only beginning to regret his "hasty action" weeks later, while on vacation in Mexico. One notes with irony that his 5th Marines commander, Ray Murray, also retired precipitously as a major general after serving as deputy commander, III Marine Amphibious Force in Vietnam, considering that war a terrible waste of marines; e-mail 12 December 2004 from Allan R. Millett. The establishment comment on Murray is that he retired for health reasons, a most Soviet judgment; cf. Edwin H. Simmons, *Over the Seawall: U.S. Marines at Inchon* (Washington: GPO, 2000), 32.

SELECTED BIBLIOGRAPHY

MANUSCRIPTS AND ARCHIVAL SOURCES

Allison, Fred H. "The Black Sheep Squadron: A Case Study in U.S. Marine Corps Developments in Close Air Support." PhD dissertation, Texas Tech University, 2003.

Craig, Edward A. "Incidents of Service 1917–1951" typescript, including twelve-page extract from field notebook, Korea. Copy in author collection; one on file at Marine Corps Recruit Depot Museum, San Diego.

Shepherd, Lemuel C. "Korean War Diary 2 July to 7 December 1950." Marine Corps University, Historical Division, Reference Section. Copy in author collection.

U.S. Army Command and General Staff College. Combined Arms Research Library Digital Library.

U.S. Far East Command. *History of the North Korean Army.* 31 July 1952. Digitized in three parts: http://cgsc.cdmhost.com/cdm4/document.php ?CISOROOT=%2Fp4013coll11&CISOPTR=811&REC=1&CISOBOX= history+of+thenorth+korean+army.

U.S. National Archives and Records Administration. Military Records Division. Record Group (RG):

RG407. U.S Army. Records of the Adjutant General's Office.

407.3. Reports Relating to World War II And Korean War Combat Operations and to Activities in Occupied Areas 1940-54.

E429. Eighth US Army, Korea (EUSAK), War Diaries, Supplementary documents; 2nd, 24th, 25th Infantry Division War Diaries, Supplementary documents.

RG127. U.S. Marine Corps.

E162. Headquarters, Marine Corps, Administrative Division, Correspondence Files 1949–50.

U.S. Marine Corps, Marine Corps University.
    Gray Research Center. Archives.
        Korea Papers.
        Oral History Collection.
        Box 55: Capt Francis I[ke] Fenton, Jr., Interview 6–9 Nov 1950
    Historical Division.
        Reference Section. Biographical files, various clipping files.
        Oral History Section. Bound Volumes.
            Lt. Gen. Edward A. Craig, 1967.
            Brig. Gen. Edward C. Dyer, 1973.
            Brig. Gen. Joseph C. Fegan, Jr.
            Maj. Gen. Raymond Murray, no date [c. 1968].

BOOKS

Appleman, Roy E. *South to the Naktong, North to the Yalu: June–November 1950*. Washington, D.C.: Office of the Chief of Military History, Department of the Army, 1961.

Berry, Henry. *Hey Mac, Where Ya Been?* New York: St Martin's Press, 1988.

Clifford, Kenneth J. *Progress and Purpose: A Developmental History of the United States Marine Corps 1900–1970*. Washington, D.C.: GPO, 1973.

Cagle, Malcolm W., and Frank A. Manson. *The Sea War in Korea*. Annapolis: Naval Institute Press, 1957.

Chapin, John C. *Fire Brigade: U.S. Marines in the Pusan Perimeter*. Washington, D.C.: Marine Corps History and Museums Division, 2000.

Drea, Edward J. *In the Service of the Emperor*. Lincoln: University of Nebraska Press, 1998.

Ent, Uzal W. *Fighting on the Brink: Defense of the Pusan Perimeter*. Paducah: Turner Publishing, 1996.

Field, James A., Jr. *History of United States Naval Operations Korea*. Washington: GPO, 1962.

Gilbert, Oscar. *Marine Corps Tank Battles in Korea*. Havertown, Pa.: Casemate, 2003.

Hammes, Thomas X. *Forgotten Warriors: The 1st Provisional Marine Brigade, the Corps Ethos and the Korean War*. Lawrence, Kans.: University Press of Kansas, 2010.

Heefner, Wilson Allen. *Patton's Bulldog: The Life and Service of General Walton H. Walker*. Shippensburg, Pa.: White Mane Publishing Company, 2002.

Keiser, Gordon W. *The U.S. Marine Corps and Defense Unification 1944–47: The Politics of Survival*. Washington, D.C.: National Defense University Press, 1982.

Knox, Donald. *The Korean War—Pusan to Chosin—An Oral History*. New York: Harcourt Brace Jovanovich, 1985.

La Bree, Clifton. *The Gentle Warrior: General Oliver Prince Smith, USMC*. Kent, Ohio: Kent State University Press, 2001.

McRae, Vincent V., and Alvin D. Coox. *Tank-vs.-Tank Combat in Korea*. Chevy Chase, Md.: Operations Research Office; The Johns Hopkins

University, 1954. Earlier version is Coox, *U.S. Armor in the Antitank Role, Korea 1950* (1952), available at http://www.kimsoft.com/2002/oro-kwarmor.pdf.

Millett, Allan R. *Semper Fidelis: The History of the United States Marine Corps.* New York: MacMillan, 1980.

———. *The War for Korea, 1945–1950: A House Burning.* Lawrence, Kans.: University Press of Kansas, 2005.

———. *The War for Korea, 1950-1951: They Came from the North.* Lawrence, Kans.: University Press of Kansas, 2010.

Montross, Lynn, and Nicholas A. Canzona. *U.S. Marine Operations in Korea.* Vol. 1, *The Pusan Perimeter.* Washington: Historical Branch, G-3, Marine Corps, 1954.

Munroe, Clark C. *The Second United States Infantry Division in Korea 1950–51.* Tokyo: Toppan Printing Co., 1951.

Parker, Gary W., and Frank M. Batha, Jr. *A History of Marine Observation Squadron Six.* Washington: Marine Corps History and Museums Division, HQMC, 1982.

Robertson, William Glenn. *Counterattack on the Naktong, 1950.* No. 13 in *Leavenworth Papers.* Ft. Leavenworth: Combat Studies Institute, 1985.

Ross, Steven T. *American War Plans 1945–1950.* London: Frank Cass, 1996.

Shaw, Jr., Henry I. *The United States Marines in North China 1945–1949.* Washington, D.C.: Headquarters, U.S. Marine Corps, 1960.

Sloan, Bill. *The Darkest Summer: Pusan and Inchon 1950, the Battles that Saved South Korea—and the Marine Corps—from Extinction.* New York: Simon & Schuster, 2009.

Slater, Michael. *Hills of Sacrifice: The 5th RCT in Korea.* Paducah: Turner Publishing, 2000.

Taplett, Robert D. *Dark Horse Six.* Williamstown, N.J.: Phillips Publishing, 2002.

Terry, Addison. *The Battle for Pusan: A Korean War Memoir.* Novato: Presidio, 2000.

The Marine Corps Reserve, A History. Washington, D.C.: Headquarters, U.S. Marine Corps, 1966.

Y'Blood, William T. *The Three Wars of Lt. Gen. George E. Stratemeyer: His Korean War Diary.* Washington D.C.: GPO, 1999.

ARTICLES

Durand, James F. "The Ghost-Catching Marines: The ROKMC before the Inchon Landing." *Marine Corps Gazette* 84 (September, 2000), 94–101.

Fenton, Francis I., Jr. "Changellon Valley." *Marine Corps Gazette* 35 (November 1951) : 43–53.

Giusti, Ernest H. "Marine Air Over the Pusan Perimeter." *Marine Corps Gazette* 36 (May 1952): 18–27.

Manza, John D. "The First Provisional Marine Brigade in Korea." Pts. 1 and 2. *Marine Corps Gazette* 84 (July and August 2000): 66–74 and 82–89.

Millett, Allan R. "A Reader's Guide to the Korean War." *Journal of Military History* 61 (July 1997): 583–597.

INDEX